It's martial. It's mental judo. Where you use the other guy's energy to win. It's mind-set. It's charisma.... [A] non-threatening approach that in many ways builds on the principles laid out long ago in Dale Carnegie's How to Win Friends and Influence People.

—*New York Times* Description of Bob
Mayer's Winning Methodology

Getting things to go your way: Bob Mayer tells you what to say and how to say it. This is the kind of book we all badly need but seldom see.

—Richard Freedman, Retired CEO, Pottery Barn Inc.

Robert Mayer skillfully and with masterful prose guides us along the path to powerful persuasion. The journey is made more meaningful because Mayer is, in fact, a master of persuasion strategy. Prepare to be enlightened with the turn of every page.

—Kathleen Kelley Reardon, University of Southern California
Marshall School of Business Professor and Author
of *The Skilled Negotiator: Mastering the
Language of Engagement*

A persuasion pro guides us on an empowering journey through the "mind-field." Along the way, you'll hit rich lodes of tested and proven ready-to-go tips and plays designed to impact and influence the decisions other people make.

—Rob Kautz, President and CEO, Wolfgang Puck
Worldwide, Inc.

HOW TO

WITHOUT RAISING YOUR VOICE,

WIN ANY

LOSING YOUR COOL,

ARGUMENT

OR COMING TO BLOWS.

ROBERT MAYER

CAREER
PRESS

Franklin Lakes, NJ

HOW TO WIN ANY ARGUMENT
EDITED AND TYPESET BY GINA M. CHESELKA
Cover design by Mada Design Inc./NYC
Printed in the U.S.A. by Book-mart Press

To order this title, please call toll-free 1-800-CAREER-1 (NJ and Canada: 201-848-0310) to order using VISA or MasterCard, or for further information on books from Career Press.

CAREER
PRESS

The Career Press, Inc., 3 Tice Road, PO Box 687,
Franklin Lakes, NJ 07417
www.careerpress.com

Library of Congress Cataloging-in-Publication Data

Mayer, Robert,
    How to win any argument : without raising your voice, losing your
cool, or coming to blows / by Robert Mayer.
      p. cm.
    Includes index.
    ISBN 1-56414-810-6 (pbk.)
    1. Interpersonal conflict. I. Title.

BF637.I48M4 2005
153.6--dc22

                 2004063219

Dedication

Dedicated with love to the memory of my parents, Anne and Franc Mayer, whose "do the right thing" social conscience continues to be an inspiration.

To my beautiful wife, Beverly, for her love; affection; and gentle, caring spirit. To Melissa, Steve, Michelle, Aaron, Zachary, and Gail.

And to Frederick J. Glassman, a great friend and law partner.

Acknowlegments

Thanks to Michael Snell for your no-holds-barred advice and right-on marketing savvy. You have mastered the art of being a truly great agent.

And thanks to Karl Weber, who, as my *Power Plays* editor at Random House, agreed with me that a "how-to" book could be an entertaining page-turner, and at the same time a highly informative guide.

Table of Tactics

Introduction

Because you'll want to meet the blonde guy with the tuna melt and fries

Think about your last argument with a family member, a coworker, a supplier, a customer, a boss, a contractor, or the IRS.

Were you convinced the other side had a closed mind? Did either side put up the same tired arguments, resisting new facts and information? Did either side overgeneralize their differences, saying, "You always," "You only," or "You never"? Did either side make threats they really didn't want to carry out? Did either side lose their cool? Did the other side then counter by angrily raising his or her voice?

Arguments are a war of words...

Each side digging in to defend their position. Resisting change because they are committed to the status quo...*or* because in their mind there is a justification that supports their position...*or* because they are attached to what is comfortable and familiar...*or* because their good judgment is on the line.

Each side withholding information or distorting the information they choose to give. Each side saying only those things they can say well. Each side changing from being stubbornly right to being adamantly righteous. Each side relying on their gut instincts and premonitions. And why not? It's always easier to take a stand than to understand. So, too, it's easier to decide against than to decide for.

As the war of words wages on, issues become more complex. Outcomes become less predictable. Retorts become more simplistic.

11

Or maybe there is silence—the hardest argument of all to refute. And so it is.

This book teaches you a better way. Winning arguments without quarreling, squabbling, tussling, wrangling, bickering, raising your voice, losing your cool, or coming to blows. Winning arguments without bulldozing and browbeating the other guy. Winning arguments by finessing rather than forcing, kickin' butt, or being in the other guy's face.

You'll learn how to make, manage, and move arguments without offending or embarrassing anyone, including yourself. How to win arguments with confidence, grace, and ease.

The art of argument. It's mysterious and powerful. It's the art of having things go your way. And the art of getting out of your own way. It's having "the moves." But it's also having "the touch."

You'll learn the way of the ancient martial arts masters. In Japanese, *ju* means "gentle," *do* means "way." *Judo* means "gentle way." The gentle way is directing rather than confronting the other guy's energy. But what you're about to discover won't turn you into a softie.

Winning isn't about pushy pitches, dolling up your ideas with rouge and rhinestones, or having a gift of gab. The winning way is to *get a grip*, because you need to be in control of how you will be. To construct a *Consent Zone*, because you need to manage emotions, not avoid them. To *link*, because you need things to *feel right* so a person *will* or *want* to follow your lead. To *lead* with bulletproof reasoning, because what you say needs to *sound right*. And to *cinch consent*, because in the end you want to trigger action.

There are reasons why all of us do what we do. The reasons don't have to be good reasons—they often aren't. The reasons don't have to be the product of conscious choice—they often aren't. This is a book about being people savvy. Understanding what makes people—including ourselves—tick.

You will discover what works—and what doesn't—when you are up against a stone wall...*or* when your ideas are being rejected...*or* when you are confronted with hostility and anger. You'll learn how to be an uncompromising compromiser. How to finesse people who would rather be right than reasonable and stand up to people you can't stand.

Along with the moves for outgunning and outmaneuvering the other guy, you'll learn techniques for developing life skills that will dramatically enhance your chances of professional success and personal satisfaction.

Before we get started, here are a few folks I'd like you to meet...

Meet Karen From Modesto
Because there are arguments about getting engaged

"My boyfriend and I have been going together for six years. We argue about when we're getting engaged. I'm for sooner. He's for sometime in the undefined future."

It was my first book. My first radio interview. My first on-the-air telephone-in listener. With a half million or so northern California listeners tuned in, Karen had jump-started my book tour.

The show quickly took Karen off the air, saying it was unfair for her to dump her question on me rather than an advice-to-the-lovelorn columnist.

A few weeks after Karen's call, I was invited to speak at Tulane University. An MBA class said Karen's question was fair. One hour and two cups of chicory coffee later, I was speaking to a class of third-year law students. The law students disagreed with the MBA students. As a member of the Great Loophole Industry, I know that law students are programmed to disagree with everything. Sorry, law students, but I'm siding with the MBAs.

Arguing for a desired outcome is part of every relationship, including our most intimate ones. What you're about to discover isn't about making you a more effective businessperson or more effective leader. It's about making you a more effective person, whether you're a Fortune 500 CEO or a PTA secretary. Whether you're revered or ignored. Whether your style is chess or poker. A person soliciting donations or soliciting votes. A staffer who has been given the task of crafting a knock-'em-dead proposal. A speaker striving for assent or a manager arguing for consent. Or Karen, a woman from Modesto, arguing that it's about time to make it permanent.

Meet Ken
Because he says I'm teaching you to be manipulative

Professional con artists and top-gun lawyers. Superstars selling Beverly Hills mansions, and a fire-and-brimstone evangelist selling God. Political speech writers, professional fundraisers, and psychology gurus. I met with and collected tips, tricks, and tactics from good guys and bad guys having but one thing in common: in their own respective arena, each is an Impresario of Influence, a Master of Persuasion. It is to that mix that I added my own experiences as a been-there, done-that mediator and lawyer.

"Bob, aren't you really teaching people how to be manipulative?"

Ken was a New York call-in radio show listener who didn't mince words.

Ken, please notice that the title of this book isn't *How to Stick It to Other People by Tricking Them Out of Their Money and Most Cherished Possessions.*

Al Smith, like Ken, was a New Yorker. When he was governor back in the 1920s, he was asked how he felt about prohibition and the consumption of alcohol—hot political topics of the day. His response was classic:

> If by alcohol you mean that which is the defiler of innocence, the corrupter of chastity, the scourge of disease, the ruination of the mind and the cause of unemployment and broken families, then of course I oppose it with every resource of mind and body.
>
> But if by alcohol you mean that spirit of fellowship; that oil of conversation which adds lilt to the lips and music to the mouth; that liquid warmth which gladdens the soul and cheers the heart; that benefit whose tax revenue has contributed countless millions into public treasuries to educate our children, to care for the blind, and treat our needy elder citizens—then with all the resources of my mind and body I favor it.

What you're about to discover is an art that can build or destroy. An art whose skillful application can be used to promote intolerance or to fight for better schools.

Meet the Blonde Guy With the Tuna Melt and Fries
Because duct tape isn't a solution

The tables at Ruby's Diner are pretty close together, so I couldn't help overhearing the conversation one table over.

The blonde guy with the tuna melt and fries was having a car problem. For the last three days, the red warning light on his instrument panel wouldn't go out.

"Well, you've got two choices. Either you get it fixed, or cover the light with a piece of duct tape," his friend suggested.

Relationships—whether brief or long-term; whether business, family, or social—are seldom glide-path smooth. Life's avenues aren't without potholes. Conflict is an inescapable part of the human condition.

The choice is yours: You can keep on driving as if conflict and glitches will somehow magically self-remedy. Or you can smooth the course by putting into play what you'll learn on our journey that's about to begin.

So find yourself a comfortable chair. Pour yourself a cup of coffee. Sit back, relax. By the way, don't go looking for charts, graphs, or boring stats. You won't find any psychobabble here. I've tried to make our journey entertaining as well as informative. Let me know if I've succeeded. My Website is *www.TheWayToWin.net.*

Let's get started!

CHAPTER

1

Gain Absolute and Total Self-Control

Because winning begins by controlling how you will be

What separates the amateurs from the pros is self-mastery. How you walk the valleys. How you maneuver the turns. How you're able to get out of your own way.

In this chapter you'll discover the empowering secret of a *still center*.

Meet David

Because he knows the secrets of the Ancient Masters

> *Mastering others requires force. Mastering the self needs strength.*
>
> —The *Tao Te Ching*

You won't find a single Maharishi U. sweatshirt hanging in my closet. I have never recited Zen Buddhist *koans*, tried to be in touch with my *chi* energy, or experienced the great light show.

I'm a khaki and leather laces utilitarian. A reality based, prove-it-to-me kind of guy.

Nonetheless...

17

Even more impressive than David's credentials (former university professor and law school dean) was his style. How he handled himself in days of end-to-end meetings. His acute awareness and the subtle things he picked up on. How he easily overcame resistance and at the same time galvanized us all. How he knew exactly what to say. And his special sense of how and when to say it. How David got others to feel what he felt. Believe what he believed. Think what he thought.

I later discovered that David's way was the way of the ancient Asian masters....

The Ancient Masters were subtle, mysterious, profound, responsive.

Watchful, like men crossing a winter stream.

Alert, like men of danger.

Courteous, like visiting guests.

What I'm about to share with you may sound like a mantra from a misty mountaintop. But if you're willing to be unconditionally receptive, you too will discover why David's style is so effective.

Are you ready?

Take a few slow, deep breaths.

Imagine that deep within you there's an *oasis of inner calm*. Imagine, too, a *dimension of detached awareness*. A dimension that makes it possible to see things from the vantage of a player on the field as well as an observer on the sidelines.

To imagine is to self-empower. You have just actualized what the Ancient Masters sought—*a still center*.

Now...

Imagine having the power to be aware of how you feel. ("I feel hostile because...." "I feel angry because....")

Imagine having the power to *respond* rather than *react*. When you react, the event controls you. When you respond, you are in control. How you choose to perceive a situation will often determine its outcome.

Imagine having the power to control your anger and emotions. To be aware of your gut impulses. ("What he is saying makes me want to....") To be able to lower your voice as others are raising theirs.

Imagine having the power to be aware of the risks and consequences of giving way to your impulses. ("If I give into my impulses, then what will probably happen is....")

Imagine having the power to separate what is important from what is urgent. The power to pause. To observe. To absorb before acting. To be aware of alternative solutions and their benefits. ("The best thing would be for me to....")

• • • •

Nick, a Midwestern television station manager, invited me back to his office after an on-the-set interview. The plaque on Nick's wall somehow said it all:

*Every morning in Africa, a gazelle wakes up knowing
it must run faster than the lion or be killed.*

*Every morning, a lion awakens knowing it must
outrun the slowest gazelle or starve to death.*

It doesn't matter if you are a lion or a gazelle.

When the sun comes up, you'd better be running.

Nick's plaque can be summed up in three words: *business as usual.* Confrontations with people who will argue about anything. Or even worse, who will argue about nothing. Confrontations with people who argue because they would rather be right than reasonable. The bossy. The "boo leaders" who reject your ideas before you've had a chance to develop them. The bozos. The insensitive. The arrogant. The exhausting. People we dread having to talk to. People who drain our energy quarreling. People who make us feel anxious when they leave a message for us to call them back. People who cause us to be more self-critical in their presence.

If you have a job without conflict, then you don't really have a job. Each of us has aggravation. Problems. Frustrations. Each of our lives is made up of peaks and valleys, twists and turns. There'll be days you'll play hopscotch with unicorns. Days when you'll play Tokyo to your boss's Godzilla. What makes us different from each other is how we walk the valleys, how we maneuver the turns. How we carry the load. You can't always control the conflict, but with a *still center* you can always control your *reaction* to it.

In the morning the sun will come up again. Nick, I'm not telling you you'll be able to stop the race. But I do promise that as you discover the way to win, you'll become one hell of a runner.

Heads Up

Absolute and total self-control flows from a *still center.* Having a still center doesn't mean you'll always be in total control of the conflict itself. It means you'll always be in total control of your *reaction* to it.

---

7 Ways a Still Center Keeps You From Getting in Your Own Way

Knowing others is wisdom. Knowing the self is enlightenment.

—The *Tao Te Ching*

1. You Get in Your Own Way When You're Acting Under the Influence

Did your old grey suit (the one whose trousers have a shiny seat) suddenly become an almost-new designer model when you made a lost luggage claim at the airport? Did your tax return overvalue the long-obsolete stereo and computer equipment that you donated to Goodwill? Do you skate on moral thin ice by saying, "But everyone does it"?

Your answers to these questions...the future of affirmative action...the rights and wrongs of abortion...gay marriage..the role of America's military and economic might...the style of shock jock Howard Stern...human cloning...the legalization of marijuana...the death penalty—how you see things big and small is shaped by your influences.

Who influences us has segued from psychology guru Dr. Spock to *Star Trek*'s Mr. Spock. From Beaver Cleaver to Beavis and Butt-Head (the television stars who introduced the word *ass-munch* to the prepubescent vernacular). From Ozzie Nelson (early television's *Adventures of Ozzie and Harriet*) to Ozzy Osbourne (*The Osbournes*).

We are influenced by Howard Stern's Fartman and *South Park*'s Cartman, a cartoon flatulent third grader. (One episode of this cable show is titled "Cartman's Mom Is a Dirty Slut.") And we are influenced by the outcomes of the O.J. Simpson trials and by the Simpsons, a dysfunctional cartoon family. (In one typical display of Simpson-style parenting, Homer Simpson told his daughter Lisa that it's proper to steal "from people you don't like.")

At the FBI Academy, agents are taught that everybody is *AUI*—"acting under the influence."

Here's what I learned about being AUI from a lobster and hot dog dinner...

On the *USS Helena*, officers planned the meals for the ship's sailors. The only restriction was the mess hall budget. A group of us shavetail ensigns (Navy-talk for wet-behind-the-ears, newly commissioned officers) were walking through the mess hall one evening when we heard a sailor tell a food server, "Give me a whole lot of that brown stuff." The sailor's "mystery meat" request launched what we thought was a "great plan."

Our plan was to skimp here and there. To build a budget reserve for one awesome meal. A meal that would have the crew dining instead of just nowing down. The entrée that would have the Pacific Fleet talking for weeks to come would be broiled lobster tails with sweet drawn butter. For those who didn't eat seafood, there would be a tried-and-true standby: hot dogs and beans.

The surprise was ours, the know-it-alls with the gold collar bars and the great plan. Over 90 percent of the crew opted for the hot dogs and beans!

In a volunteer Navy, many of the enlisted personnel are from small towns, farms, and parts of big cities where lobster tails aren't part of the gastronomical experience. Few knew that lobster was a pricey delicacy. And to our disappointment, they really didn't care.

Not too long ago, I was negotiating the purchase of a palatial beachfront house for my client. It was once owned by one of Hollywood's biggest stars. The asking price was $8 million. When we were within a hundred thousand dollars or so of making a deal, the seller said, "I will accept your offer to buy if we close the sale in March, but you let me use the garden in May to entertain my East Coast relatives." The seller was AUI. He had an emotional need to show the house to his relatives who had not yet been west.

Brian, our remodeling contractor, had just installed a new sink, lighting system, and appliances in our kitchen. At the end of the day, the kitchen was filled with old copper tubing, soda cans, Styrofoam, sandwich wrappings, plastic bags, and boxes or refuse that Brian meticulously separated and deposited into three types of recycling trash containers.

Brian seemed to be a true friend of the environment. But when I walked Brian to his truck, I saw that it had Ohio license plates. Knowing he lived and worked in Los Angeles, I just had to ask why. "I keep it registered in Ohio. That way I don't have to comply with California's strict air quality emissions requirements. None of those damn smog checks for me," he said. Brian, too, was AUI.

While we're talking trash…

No matter how hard I try, there's a lot of modern art that I'll never understand. But then I'm not alone. Artist Gustav Metzger had his work readied for display at Tate Modern, London's famed art museum. The day before the exhibit opened, a janitor threw out a bag of garbage that was incorporated as an integral part of Metzger's artwork. The cleaner said he thought it was trash. We are all AUI. And one man's throw-away trash is part of another man's celebrated artwork.

Some historical examples…

Ford Motor Company was AUI. It didn't run any Lincoln-Mercury ads in the *New Yorker* for six months. The magazine's offense? It ran a rock and rap article adjacent to a Mercury advertisement. The article quoted sexually graphic song lyrics from the group Nine Inch Nails.

Omega watches was AUI. It pulled its advertising from British *Vogue*. It didn't want to be in a magazine that featured "skeletal" models of "anorexic proportions." Omega found it "extremely distasteful" to idealize slenderness so extreme that it encouraged real women to hate their own bodies.

Redbook was AUI. It was concerned how its subscribers would react to a cover featuring Pierce Brosnan and his then girlfriend, and now wife, as she breast-fed their son. *Redbook*'s editor saw "tenderness in the photo." But she also knew there are "some people who are uncomfortable with breast-feeding. I didn't want to force that on anyone who is a subscriber." The solution: Two different *Redbook* covers were printed. The newsstand edition shows mom breast-feeding, while subscribers got a picture of the couple simply holding the baby.

Titleist golf balls was AUI. It wasn't warned by *Sports Illustrated* that the magazine was running an article on how the Dinah Shore Golf Tournament in Palm Springs had become the unofficial annual "spring break" for an estimated 20,000 lesbians. Calling the article "inexcusable," Titleist cancelled more than $1 million in advertising.

Sears was AUI. Benetton is an international brand of upscale clothing that injected social issues into its advertising. There was the Benetton cloud of multicolored condoms poster and the poster featuring a priest kissing a nun. There was the ad whose message was peace and brotherhood. It featured a black horse and a white horse mating. And there were the "We, of Death Row" anti-capital punishment ads that featured the faces of prisoners condemned to die. Enough was enough already—Sears pulled all Benetton products off its shelves.

Heads Up

You're AUI. Your influences are a part of what makes you tick. A *still center* empowers you to be less reactive to influences. To be more analytical. To step back and make sense of your motives and priorities—your influences.

---

2. You Get in Your Own Way When You See Things the Way You Want Them to Be

Renewing my driver's license was a traumatic experience. My test answers were right on. It was the application's hair color question that I blew.

I look at myself in the mirror every morning. I have always had brown hair. But the clerk who took my application looked me over, whited-out "brown," and quickly typed in "grey."

"Hey, my hair is brown," I insisted.

The clerk fired back, "You don't have brown hair—you are mostly grey with some strands of brown here and there."

My mirror reflected what I wanted to see.

Heads Up

You see things the way you want them to be. A *still center* empowers you to look at yourself without your rose-colored Ray-Bans. Knowing your real strengths and weaknesses helps you manage both more powerfully.

---

3. You Get in Your Own Way When You Color the World With Your Expectations

We don't want to change the way we view the world. That's why we'll do almost anything to cling to cherished notions. The country's reaction to the My Lai incident is historical proof that sometimes the result is truly ludicrous.

Charlie Company's 150 soldiers, led by Lieutenant William Calley, stormed into the Vietnamese village of My Lai. The My Lai bloodbath went on for four hours. There was no resistance from the villagers.

When it was over...

> Number of Viet Cong soldiers encountered at My Lai: 0.
>
> Number of civilian villagers killed: 504.
>
> Number of American casualties: 1 (a soldier shot himself in the foot).
>
> Number of weapons confiscated from the villagers: 3.

In the subsequent court martial, Lt. Calley was found guilty of murder and sentenced to life in prison for his part in the murder of 22 civilians. After he'd served three days in prison, Calley was moved to Fort Benning, Georgia, where he was held under house arrest in a comfortable apartment.

Many couldn't believe that Calley was anything other than a hero in the struggle against communist aggression. A record, "The Battle Hymn of Lieutenant Calley," became a modest hit. Protest rallies were staged on his behalf. Several state legislatures passed resolutions seeking clemency. After having served three years under house arrest, he was pardoned. Calley later went on the college lecture circuit at $2,000 a speech and appeared on the cover of *Esquire* surrounded by Asian children.

Why and how could this happen? In 1968, we expected and wanted to believe that American boys are always just and righteous. What happened at My Lai was inconsistent with our expectations and what we wanted to believe. Have your expectations changed in light of the abuses inflicted on detainees by a handful of U.S. military personnel at Iraq's Abu Ghraib prison in 2003?

> ### Heads Up
> You color the world with your expectations. You tend to accept as credible any evidence that supports your beliefs. So, too, you give short shrift to evidence that contradicts or challenges what you believe. A *still center* empowers you to consider "the why"—why you believe what you believe.

4. You Get in Your Own Way When You Conclude Facts from Your Assumptions

A Beverly Hills perfume shop's sign read, "COMPARE OUR PRICES TO DUTY-FREE SHOP PRICES." After looking around the store, I told the clerk that even though they thought their prices were less than duty-free, they were mistaken. "We didn't say they were less. Our sign only says compare prices," she responded.

> ### Quick Quiz
> Four paperback volumes of Sherlock Holmes mysteries are standing on a shelf in sequential order. Each volume is 2-inches thick.
>
> A bookworm in a straight line eats his way from page one of Volume I to the last page of Volume IV. How many inches of Sherlock Holmes mysteries did the bookworm eat?
>
> *The answer in a minute...*

Here's a favorite workshop question of mine. Let's see how you do...

Joe is 30 years old. He is very shy and withdrawn, with little real interest in people or the world of reality. A meek and tidy soul, he has a need for order and structure, and has a passion for detail. Is it more likely that Joe is a salesman or a librarian?

Two-thirds of the executives who were asked about Joe pegged him as a librarian. But there are 75 times as many salespeople in the United States as there are librarians. Statistically, the greater chance is that Joe is a salesman. Just because something seems probable, doesn't make it so.

Maybe you made a fatal assumption about Joe. If so, you're in good company. Look at the fatal assumptions Wal-Mart made...

Wal-Mart built U.S.-style parking lots for its shopping centers in Mexico. But most citizens there don't own cars. City bus stops were behind the seemingly endless lots, making it a tough haul for shoppers to get their purchases home.

In Latin America, Sam's Club (Wal-Mart's discount food operation) fizzled and flopped. Shoppers who lived in cramped apartments didn't buy— or have room for—its huge multipack items.

In Brazil, Wal-Mart designed stores with U.S.-size aisles. Aisles that couldn't accommodate the crush of shoppers who did the bulk of their shopping once a month on pay day.

And look at the fatal assumptions you make about Wal-Mart...

You assume there will be a discount for large purchases you make at Wal-Mart. Value in value-sizes. At a Wal-Mart in Mesa, Arizona, a savvy reporter discovered that the 64-ounce Heinz catsup was 25 percent more per ounce than the smaller bottle. The 16-ounce Minute Maid frozen orange juice was 51 percent more per ounce than the smaller size. The family-size container of Cool Whip was more per ounce than the tub half its size. At a Chicago Wal-Mart, two single canisters of Pringles were cheaper than the "Twin Pack" Pringles. None of the items priced by the reporter were on sale or promotion.

• • • •

Note: You're not ready to read past this line until you've taken the Quick Quiz on page 25.

The answer to the bookworm quiz is 4 inches. How can that be? Page one of Volume I when standing on a shelf is on the *far right* of Volume I. The last page of Volume IV when standing on a shelf is on the *far left* of Volume IV. The bookworm only ate through Volumes II and III. If you were wrong, it's because you made a false assumption.

But don't feel bad. Fewer than 10 percent of workshop students correctly answer the bookworm quiz. This is true even when the workshop is for executives and managers!

Heads Up

You conclude facts from your assumptions. You quickly accept the intuitive as conclusive. The apparent as real. You make assumptions about others. About facts. About circumstances. Your reality—what you believe—is largely based on your assumptions. A *still center* empowers you to consider whether there is a sound basis for your assumptions.

5. You Get in Your Own Way When You're Convinced That You "Know What You Know"

Quick Quiz

Okay, all you "foodies." Here's a chance to show your stuff.

Texas barbecue specials are five times more common in Atlanta than in Dallas. True or False?

You are more likely to find corned beef lunch specials in Dallas than in New York. True or False?

Deep-dish pizza specials are seven times more common in Miami restaurants than in Chicago. True or False?

Stand by for the answers...

The late Roberto Goizueta, CEO of the Coca-Cola Company, reported to his shareholders:

> After I spoke to a group of students at my alma mater, one of them asked me a simple question: which area of the world offers the Coca-Cola Company its greatest growth potential? Without hesitation, I replied "southern California." They all laughed, thinking I was trying to be funny. So to drive home the point, I shared with them one

very interesting fact. The per capita consumption of bottles and cans of Coca-Cola is actually lower in southern California than it is in Hungary. The students went silent.

Casinos take advantage of you being convinced you "know what you know" with ads touting big slot-machine payoffs. ("Highest payback." "98% return.") What isn't disclosed that often is that only one or two machines—in a casino with as many as 1,500—are that liberal.

Foster's, a major Australian brewery, was convinced that it knew what it knew when it decided to take on China's beer market in 1993. And why not? There were 1.2 billion Chinese, and beer consumption in China in the 10 preceding years had increased tenfold. The Foster's folk figured that if they sold beer to only 2 percent of the Chinese, they'd have a new market as big as its Australian market. Five years and $70 million in losses later, Foster's pulled out of China.

So what went wrong? Because Foster's knew what it knew, it under-estimated local competition in a country where it was prestigious for towns big and small to have their own brand of beer. Foster's didn't take into full account the degree to which local governments work to support hometown breweries. Nor did Foster's consider that on an everyday basis, the Chinese wouldn't pay a premium for a foreign beer.

Morrie F. is a con artist. He is in the business of selling distributor-ships. Here's how he dupes his customers who know what they know: Morrie will sell you an exclusive territory to sell wall-mounted garage storage racks. Your territory will have 500,000 homes with garages. The customer-installed storage units will sell for $195. Your cost is $80. Morrie points out two things that are true: There is nothing else quite like these racks on the market. And everyone can use more storage space.

Morrie tells you that it's reasonable to expect that 3 percent of the homeowners will want to buy a storage unit. Three in a 100—seems as easy as fishing in a trout pond. If you sell 15,000 units (3 percent of 500,000) and realize a profit of $115 each, you will make—hold tight to your hat—$1,725,000! Even if you spend $225,000 for advertising, that's a profit of $1.5 million. Now that's something to write home about.

Morrie's 3 percent seems pretty reasonable. His math is faultless. But Morrie's entire scenario is based upon a dubious premise—that 3 percent of the homeowners will be your customers. A premise readily accepted by Morrie's customers who know what they know.

Over the years, I've seen other clients lose money on "sure things" because all a boutique project needed to break even was just three customers an hour or in a restaurant project only 20 diners a meal.

What you "know" is a precursor to how you will react and respond to others and their ideas.

And lest I forget, according to *Forbes*, the answers to the three quiz questions on page 27 are true!

Heads Up

You give undue credence to what you do know, and you figure that what you don't know isn't that important. Much of what you "know" to be true is questionable, incomplete, or downright false. Yet the reality in your head is as important—as "real" to you—as the facts on the ground.

A *still center* empowers you to consider whether you really know what you know.

---

6. You Get in Your Own Way When You're Influenced by Head-Turning Tie-Ins

My in-laws don't refer to the things they bought on vacation—a cup and saucer, a carving, a wall hanging—as souvenirs or mementos. Instead they refer to these objects as "memories."

I think Fran and Lou's expression makes a lot of sense.

A handcrafted brass letter opener prompts my memories of an afternoon walking the cobblestoned streets of Budapest. That shady spot in my yard brings back memories of the great times my kids had with Casey, our Wheaton Terrier, who attained the status of a family member. Violets bring back lump-in-my-throat memories of my mother's birthdays.

Many times your feelings about an idea are because of what or whom you associate with it. The *tie-in* doesn't need to be rational, consequential, or relevant. An example: A supplier takes you to a great concert. Subconsciously you let your positive feelings about the concert tie in to how you feel about the supplier.

Here are some head-turning tie-in examples involving famous people and well-known situations. Did any of them influence how you feel about a place, person, or product?

Credibility head-turners

Cal Ripken, Jr. holds the major league record for the most consecutive baseball games played (2,632). He was also featured in an ad for Merck & Co.'s hypertension drug Prinivil: "Cal Ripken, Jr. and Prinivil….Both on the job. Every day." In small print, the ad says, "Cal Ripken, Jr. is not hypertensive and is not taking Prinivil." If the spokesperson is Cal Ripken, Jr., the product takes on an aura of durability and reliability.

Golf genius Tiger Woods plugs American Express. "It's natural for people to see an affinity between the values that Tiger represents and the values that American Express represents. We are both very focused on earned success, discipline, hard work, achievement, and integrity," boasted the president of American Express.

Michael Jordan has pitched Nike shoes and apparel, Wilson sporting goods, Hanes underwear, WorldCom telephone service, Oakley sunglasses, Rayovac batteries, Wheaties cereal, Gatorade, and Coca-Cola. Maybe Jordan is right that Wheaties are good for me. But how credible is nutrition advice from a guy who also said I should be drinking Coke? The tie-in response of marketing gurus: "Who else is cooler than Michael Jordan? Nobody today better embodies the American spirit."

Nostalgia head-turners

A poll revealed that most San Franciscans have never tried Rice-A-Roni. Nor did San Franciscans invent the rice–pasta combination dish in a box. So why is Rice-A-Roni pitched as "the San Francisco treat"? San Francisco is one of the most popular travel destinations in the country. Its fine restaurants are legendary. Rice-A-Roni trades on the strong positive feelings we have about the "City by the Bay."

The era spanning two decades after World War II is often viewed as a golden age. Communities were familiar, secure, and comfortable. We had stable jobs and relationships. An old-fashioned America when folks weren't in a hurry. Playing on the comfort of days gone by, Tulsa, Oklahoma, advertises itself as "America the way you remember it."

Moxie. About half of those who've tried it report that it tastes like cough syrup. But then Moxie is the kind of soft drink you either love or spit out. Since 1884, Moxie's fanatical faithful have found the bitter, root extract drink the "elixir of life."

While giants like Coke and Pepsi are battling for cola market share, Moxie and other obscure soft drinks are thriving in local markets across the country. These regional or "cult" brands—with down-home names like

Big Red, Sun Drop, and Kickapoo Joy Juice—developed in mostly rural areas. Consumers identify with cult brands because of their ability to evoke nostalgia and a sense of regional pride.

And is this taking advantage or what? Restaurant specials bearing the word *mom* are "on average, priced 15 percent higher than non-mom specials," reports *Forbes*.

"Being cool" or prestigious head-turners

"Steak isn't good for you, but it's still really good. In business it remains the dinner of champions. Because a steak dinner is, more than ever, a special event," observed *Fortune*.

The 170-year-old cognac brand Courvoisier has launched a line of men's and women's sportswear. An ad campaign featured pink boots, a red silk dress, and diamond earrings spelling the logo "CV".

Land Rover has cachet, but few can afford the pricey four-wheel drive vehicles. The solution? Land Rover shoes. Footwear with the Land Rover logo, according to the shoe licensee, "carries the same image of adventure, guts, and supremacy that the vehicles carry." That's why Nike's Air Zoom Ultraflight has an outer shell modeled after the engine deck on a Ferrari Modena. And why Nike's Air Jordan XVIII comes with side air flaps reminiscent of a Lamborghini's air intakes. Don't hold your breath. I don't think you'll be seeing footwear that looks like a Ford Focus.

Heads Up

Tie-ins are head-turners that influence how we think and feel. A head-turning tie-in can be as simple as a gift from a salesperson or being treated to dinner by someone soliciting your vote at an upcoming meeting. Tie-ins don't need to make sense to impact how you feel or think. A *still center* empowers you to consider whether the tie-in is relevant, appropriate, or applicable.

---

7. You Get in Your Own Way When You're Too Stubborn to Let Go of the Peanut

Tiny monkeys live along the African coast. They're fast and live high in the treetops, so there's no way to catch one unless you know the monkey hunter's secret. Africans drill a hole in a coconut that is just big enough for a monkey to squeeze his hand inside. The coconut milk is spilled out, and a peanut coated with honey is dropped into the hole. A monkey will always reach down into the hole to grab the peanut. With his fist clenched, the monkey's hand is bigger than the hole. As long as he holds onto the peanut, he can't shake free from the coconut. Because the monkey can only think of the peanut, he won't release his grip, even when the monkey hunters come to toss a net over him.

You, too, sometimes get in your own way by being so focused on a singular objective that you don't let go of the peanut.

Legend tells of a samurai warrior whose life's quest was to avenge the brutal slaying of his beloved master at the hands of a sadistic killer. After years of searching, the samurai at long last found the killer and engaged him in a duel. When the killer realized that it was the samurai who would prevail, he leaned forward and spit in the samurai's face. The samurai suddenly stopped fighting, returned his sword to its sheath, and walked away.

The samurai's students couldn't understand. "Why did you walk away?" they asked.

"Because," he explained, "my vengeance became personal."

Empowered with a still center, the samurai was able to get out of his own way. The monkey never did.

Heads Up

You get in your own way when you stubbornly refuse to let go. A *still center* empowers you to drop the peanut.

Keep this in mind: What makes you tick also makes the other guy tick. What causes you to get in your own way also causes him to get in his own way.

Take a Lesson From a Wise King

Because there's much to be learned from a mango tree

Once upon a time in a faraway land, a wise king wanted to teach his four sons a valuable life lesson. One winter, he dispatched his oldest son to see a mango grove. As winter turned to spring, his second oldest son made the journey. The third son traveled to see the trees that summer. And in the fall, it was the youngest son's turn.

Upon the youngest boy's return, the king summoned his four sons and asked each what he had seen.

"The trees looked almost bare," reported the eldest son.

"No," argued the second son. "They are leafy and green."

"The trees I saw were blooming with clusters of tiny pink flowers," the third son reported.

"No," insisted the youngest. "They are filled with orange and yellow-red fruit."

"My sons, each of you are right, for you each saw the trees at different times," said the king.

• • • •

The lesson of the mango grove is to keep in mind that the other person and you have different frames of reference, different experiences, different ways of looking at things, different values, and in all likelihood will use different words to say the same thing.

When you're aware, you don't just look—you see. You don't just listen—you hear. When you "see" and "hear," you're in *complete attendance*.

To be in complete attendance...

1. Look and Listen for "Tells"

Body signals are clues as to how the other person is receiving what you're saying. Because the clues are largely subconscious, con men appropriately call them "tells."

Antiterrorism checkpoint personnel are trained to give more credence to tells than to the spoken word. Almost all mannerisms are important. Does she choose to sit directly across from you, indicating confidence? Or does she sit at an angle, indicating she is ill at ease? Has he removed his coat, indicating that he feels comfortable with you? Are there nods of approval? Is there head-shaking disapproval? Did you say something causing her to smile in relief?

Are his arms protectively folded across his chest? Is he showing tension through compressed lips, strained laughter, blushing, giggling, staring? Is she fidgeting? Has his tone of voice become elevated and belligerent? *Visually listening* for tells is zooming in to read the other person's fine print.

2. Look and Listen for Hidden Word Messages

Only the foolish man hears all that he hears.

—Ancient Proverb

The other person's messages can be real, true, and reliable, or they can be lures, cover-ups, and decoys. Winners see and hear more than a person's words and more than the message that person is intending to convey. Construing words literally and accepting a person's messages at face value is not effective people-reading.

A teenage girl tearfully tells her boyfriend, "It doesn't matter." Are we to believe it really doesn't matter, or that it matters a lot?

The words *incidentally*, *by the way*, and *as you already know* sound casual and incidental, but they usually introduce statements a person wants to downplay or sneak by you.

Someone tells you, "You are 100 percent correct in what you are saying, but...." Does he really feel you are 100 percent right, or is he just softening you up for the bad news?

"I'll give it my best." "I will try my hardest." These statements are clues that a person is already presupposing a high probability of failure.

Statements that start, "Don't be concerned, but..." or "You have nothing to worry about..." mean only one thing: there is something to worry about up ahead.

3. Look and Listen for Priorities

Conversations, even small talk, are never as random or disorderly as they may seem.

Quick! Make a short list of television shows. Did you list items randomly? Or did you list them in the order of your personal preference? In all probability, you will present or specify things in an order that is consistent with your own priorities or desires.

Points that you may have thought were throwaway points of secondary importance may be primary points to someone else. Learning to look and listen for what the other person considers critical will enable you to argue more effectively.

4. Look and Listen for Pronoun Clues

Somehow I just can't help myself. When I agree with the position taken by my client, I subconsciously use phrases such as *"we* just won't agree to...." But when I'm dutifully following a client's instructions that are not totally to my liking, then my subconscious inclination is to say, *"He/she* won't agree to...."

The pronouns that the other person uses are both a forecast of the response he is expecting from you and a reflection of how committed he is to his argued-for position.

> ### Heads Up
> The average person talks at the rate of about 120 words per minute, but can hear and comprehend 600 words per minute. You have the capacity to listen to the speaker's words as well as to his tells, hidden word messages, priorities, and pronoun clues. The capacity to be in what the pros call "complete attendance."

Chapter Summary

Others will react the way you act. Controlling an argument begins by controlling how you will be. Self-command calls for an inner strength that can only flow from a *still center.*

A still center empowers you to get out of your own way.

Getting out of your own way is understanding that you are *AUI.* That you see things the way you want them to be. That you color the world with your expectations and too readily accept anything that supports your expectations.

It is understanding that you conclude facts from your assumptions. That you are convinced you "know what you know." That your head is turned by *tie-ins* that may not be rational, consequential, or relevant. That sometimes you're too stubborn to let go of the peanut. And that your judgment is clouded when your argument becomes a personal war of wills.

A still center empowers you to be in *complete attendance*—to be truly aware and to truly hear.

2

Construct a Consent Zone

Because people in the zone are less resistant and more receptive to you and your ideas

> The *Consent Zone* is where you'll set the tone and mood for a no-blows argument. It's a virtual finessing place where you'll be able to elicit change without eliciting defensiveness. Where you'll hit the ground walking. Where you'll manage the other person's emotions, not avoid them.
>
> In this chapter you'll discover how to construct a Consent Zone.

Meet Ensign Mayer, Who Was the Wrong Horse for the Course

Because you want to break through

Within days of my reporting aboard for duty, the *USS Helena* set sail for Yokosuka, Japan. In anticipation of joyous nights to come, the crew posted a giant photograph of Yokosuka's Country Plus Bar in their bunkroom. The sign outside the bar read "Beers Cold, Women Ready, Whisky."

My job was to persuade the men to stay away from the "for you a special price" girls. There I was, 22 years old. A newly minted ensign.

A never-been-there/never-done-that Navy veteran of two weeks, lecturing about venereal disease and life in the fast lane. Any knowledge I had on the subject was limited to an 11th grade glance-through "reading" of Henrik Ibsen's *Hedda Gabler.*

I started to deliver my talk in quasi-clinical terms—reserved, the way a nervous father might talk to his son. I'd taken classes in public speaking and knew my message had been delivered with succinctness and clarity. In college, I would've been disappointed with less than an A for what I believed was an exemplary effort. But I wasn't in class, and Krieger, a salty boatswain's mate with 20 years in the Navy, motioned me aside and strongly suggested that he do the talking.

Krieger was able to *identify* with the men, and he broke through in a way I never could: "There'll be a lot of good-time girls waiting for you in Yokosuka, but I don't want you to touch those girls even if you're wearing two rubbers. If anybody comes back scratching, I'll personally pop them in the snot locker [Navy-speak for nose]."

Sometimes age is the winner's edge...

A marketing and consulting firm cautioned baby boomers to be ready for the fade-out of 20th-century icons, explaining, "Young people haven't shared your experiences and have different needs and heroes."

Less than half of 1 percent of people under the age of 25 name the Beatles, Bob Marley, or Jimi Hendrix among their favorite performers.

Elvis is now being marketed as a young, rebellious innovator. One rock critic didn't pull any punches: "Kids care about cool, and they see all those fat old people getting off the tourist bus to worship at Graceland. That's the antithesis of cool."

When I was a single guy, "dating" described an intimate relationship. But then came the yuppies who stopped calling it "dating." I can understand their thinking. "Dating" does sound like something from Paleontology 101: "I am dating Bev." The yuppies replaced "dating" with "going out." People with an intimate relationship were "going out." "Going out" isn't used as a frame of reference by today's singles, and has been superceded by "seeing someone," as in "I am seeing Bev."

"It's a lot more convincing than having some pinstripe talking to them," is how a MasterCard vice president explained why City Kids produced the rap video "Master Your Future" for MasterCard. The video, which is shown in high schools throughout the country, explains why maintaining a good credit history is "cool."

MXG keeps its pitch, like, y'know, authentic when it sells tank tops, platform shoes, and other teenage wardrobe musts on the Internet and in its *magalog*—part magazine, part catalogue publication. MXG hires teenage girls whose after-school job it is to respond to customer inquiries and punch up advertising copy.

Toyota had to shake off its geezer-mobile image. (After all, it's the car Mom and Dad drive.) A youth-marketing staff made up of 24- to 35-year-olds was brought aboard—and things at Toyota changed. Toyota's ad in *Teen* was a "tip" for new drivers:

> Attention nose pickers: Just because you are alone in your
> car—NEWS FLASH—you are not invisible.

Toyota—winning over America's youth with booger jokes.

At other times, gender is the winner's edge...

For Ricky Ricardo, an "ay yi yi yi yi" and a slap to his forehead said it all. Think "Lucy." Immediately you remember her for her celebrity hounding. Her off-key singing and constant scheming. And for her Ethel-befriending, Desi-imitating ways.

But Lucy Ricardo should also be remembered as TV's first feminist. A television historian wrote that *I Love Lucy* showed us something that we had never seen before on TV: That "women express themselves differently from men. They tend to focus on emotions; they seek consensus, not conflict; they disclose more of themselves in conversation; they emphasize the personal, not the impersonal."

A few years back, almost all of the managers in charge of leasing high-rise office space for their new or expanding businesses were middle-aged men. Don G. was a real estate broker who specialized in West Los Angeles's Century City office space. Don's agency became one of Century City's top leasing firms in no time flat. He did it by knowing how to play the gender card. The agents that Don hired to show space were beautiful (and smart) women. Given the choice of being shown office space by some guy wearing tasseled loafers and a blue blazer or one of Don's women, who do you think all those middle-aged male managers chose?

Heads Up

Cultural challenges. Language challenges. Personality challenges. Gender challenges. Age challenges. Perception challenges. Who should run the course? Should it be you? Or perhaps someone with whom the other person can identify?

Be a Thermostat, Not a Thermometer

Because you want to set the climate to "win"

Television history is dotted with long-running series that were not critically acclaimed. These shows, however, provided viewers with a star that audiences wanted in their homes for a long time and with whom they felt "really comfortable," commented the president of CBS Entertainment.

The cosmetic area of a department store can be intimidating and overwhelming. Estée Lauder "Beauty Advisors" are taught to turn browsers into buyers by quickly constructing a *Consent Zone*. They are coached to start with an icebreaker, such as "I just love what you're wearing," instead of the usual "May I help you?"

Are you more comfortable with someone who exudes optimism, enthusiasm, and has a laid-back way, or someone who is forever fretting?

Alex was a professional hypochondriac. I was his lawyer, not his doctor. But, nonetheless, over 20 years or so our every conference would be preceded by Alex reciting a litany of his aches and pains. Alex's venting left me feeling uncomfortable. When he died at age 80, a member of my staff suggested that Alex's gravestone read, "See! I told you I was sick!"

We all have problems. Truth is, my problems will never seem as big to you as they do to me. Nor will they ever seem as interesting, as engrossing, or as dramatic to you as they do to me. If I spend more than a few seconds laying my problems on you, you'll find being with me an uncomfortable experience.

Comfortable people are more apt to be receptive to you and your argument. More apt to hang in there and fully hear you out. More apt to track and consider your suggestions and reasoning.

Words of wisdom for the terminally professional...

Yes, it's important to come across as knowledgeable, professional, serious about your work. But there's a difference between being serious about what you do and being serious about who you are. The former is appreciated. The latter is not. Take yourself lightly—be able to laugh at yourself. See the potential for humor and creativity in every situation.

Not being a know-it-all means hearing what the other fellow has to say. He may surprise you with an idea you really like.

If you've ever been to San Diego, you've seen the El Cortez Hotel. The city's one-time crown jewel is a downtown landmark. It's easily recognized because, although the El Cortez is an older hotel, it has an outdoor glass elevator that is consistent with much newer architecture. Before the glass elevator, the hotel only had a single interior elevator to shuttle guests between their rooms and the lobby.

Remodeling experts said the only thing that could be done to add a second elevator would be to cut holes in each floor and install one. It was a plan that would have entailed a huge expense and lost income while the hotel was closed for construction. A hotel janitor mopping floors overheard the experts talking. "Why not build the elevator on the outside of the hotel?" he asked. It had never been done before, nor had the architects and engineers even considered such an idea until then. Outdoor elevators are now very much a part of the architectural scene. But the one at the El Cortez was first!

Cool It

Because "know-it-alls" don't win arguments

If God hadn't made me so beautiful, I'd be a teacher.

—Supermodel Linda Evangelista

Tulane Law School's dean confided to me:

> The trouble with young professionals, particularly newly minted lawyers and MBAs from top schools, is that they are often as smug as they are bright. They talk down to other people as if they had the seasoning that only comes from years of hands-on experience.

Take the case of a brilliant 25-year-old. He was called a "Wall Street Wizard." After he was profiled in a *New York Times* article as one of the "faces of the New York economy," he was asked to resign from the elite investment banking firm Morgan Stanley.

Describing himself in the interview as a "young affluent," he listed among his personal extravagances expensive electronic equipment, a Rolex watch, and a closetful of custom-made suits. So why the sudden resignation? The whiz kid broke his employer's strict code of conduct that "Morgan Stanley discourages...personal profiles...which focus on lifestyle: these stories could be perceived as self-aggrandizing."

It's not only grey-flannel firms such as Morgan Stanley that discourage blatant horn-tooting. Most people react negatively to would-be persuaders who grab opportunities to brag and boast.

You may be brilliant in your field—God's gift to law, medicine, real estate, gourmet cooking, what have you. Don't wear your brilliance on your sleeve. It won't win you arguments—only resentment as a know-it-all.

Don't accept your dog's admiration as conclusive evidence that you're wonderful. Are you as brilliant as you'd like to believe? Here's the test: Think 10 years in the future. Will you know a lot then that you don't know now thanks to 10 more years of experience and learning? If so, now pause to consider how much you have yet to learn. Did you find the test humbling?

When someone else blows your horn, the sound is twice as loud. The art of subtle self-promotion is quoting clients and customers or associates whom they know or whose reputation they respect. It's weaving real-life stories and case studies into your argument. Instead of proclaiming, "We're the fastest-growing company in our field," say something more easily digested. For example, "It's not a mere accident that we're the fastest-growing company in our field. The reason is...." It's giving credit to associates and others who've helped you achieve success.

Heads Up

Know when to cool it. No one is ever truly influenced by a know-it-all. Or even worse, a full-of-yourself tell-it-all. Let the other guy discover for himself why he should buy into your argument from your stories and experiential anecdotes and from the praise that others have for you.

Meet Helen Bundy

Because enthusiasm is contagious

When I was about 16, I got my first "real job"—summer stockboy and sometimes salesboy (only when all the salesmen were busy) at a small men's store.

My boss, Helen Bundy, had never owned a store, nor had she ever had a job selling. She opened her shop because of a vacancy in her family's building. Long Beach, California, was a navy town, and somehow a men's store made good sense.

Helen had a passion for her merchandise and it showed. She would greet a customer walking towards the suits, saying, "Let me show you this great-looking new suit!" Helen then invited the prospect to feel the buttery texture of the gabardine or the softness of the wool flannel. Tossing a suit over her arm, Helen would dash to the dress shirt counter. "Can you believe how great this suit looks with this shirt and tie?"

What I learned about selling I learned from Helen Bundy. I would consistently run "high book," outselling the store's old pros, who would ask customers, "You're looking for something in a suit? Are you interested in a solid color? A stripe? A glen plaid? Something in blue? Something in brown?"

The old pros were clueless. Lackluster guys with a lackluster style who never picked up on Helen's powerful secret: Enthusiasm is something you can feel right down to your toes. It's contagious. It sells. It seduces. It excites.

Is that an ab-machine collecting dust in your garage? And up there on your kitchen shelf...what is that—a Chop-o-Matic? A Dial-o-Matic? A Veg-o-Matic? A Mince-o-Matic? Did you buy it through an infomercial, use it a couple of times, then store it away? Or worse, never use it at all?

It's no wonder. You can't miss them and they're hard to resist—those bouncy, in-your-face infomercials that extol the virtues of everything from a Mr. MegaMemory course to GLH Formula Number 9 Hair Thickener. And of course there is that studio audience—those regular-looking folks who are often paid to feign enthusiasm.

My brother-in-law, Dr. Eliot Phillipson, was invited by his son's elementary school teacher to participate in a class program on "what people do." Later, Eliot wrote an article about his experience in the University of Toronto's Department of Medicine's newsletter. From Eliot's article:

I decided to speak about scientific research and to demonstrate how it is done. The students were extremely enthusiastic about the presentation and overflowed with questions and ideas for "future research." I was quite confident that, when put to a vote, most of the students would opt for a career in biomedical research. A few weeks later the teacher informed me that when the students voted on what they would like to do in the future, biomedical research was ranked second. Ranked first was the retailing of double-glazed windows! The children had been tremendously impressed by the parent who was in the business of manufacturing, distributing, and installing double-glazed windows. A cynic might argue that the "double-glazed parent" was merely a smooth, glossy salesman. But his key to winning over the students was an infectious interest in the subject, which he shared with clarity, and enthusiasm, and relevance.

Heads Up

Inspired enthusiasm is contagious. If you're not enthusiastic about the merits of your argument, your lack of conviction will be both apparent and contagious.

Meet Dodi Fayed

Because showing appreciation makes the other person less resistant

As everyone knows, Diana, Princess of Wales, and the man with whom she finally found happiness, Dodi Fayed, were killed when their chauffeur-driven Mercedes hit pole 13 in a Paris underpass.

Dodi Fayed was a longtime client of mine. I found him to be a likeable guy who was always appreciative of the work I did for him. Dodi's gratitude was shown in many different ways. Sometimes it was a simple "thank you." At other times it was a smoked salmon he had specially flown in from

Scotland or a gigantic food package shipped from Harrods, his family's store in London.

A few months before his death, he asked me to negotiate the purchase of a home—Julie Andrews's former Malibu beachfront compound. It was an enormous task that came to fruition just before Diana and Dodi became lovers.

Dodi needed to know that he and Di would be able to enjoy their Malibu days free from intrusive paparazzi. Extra security had been put in place, and more was being planned. We even talked of Dodi acquiring two Rottweiler guard dogs, one of whom he would name "Bob."

Appreciation can take many forms. Dodi somehow knew that I would have been pleased to share my name with a guard dog, and I told him so just a few days before he was killed.

I once overheard a handful of our firm's younger lawyers visiting with each other. The topic: Who were their favorite clients? The ones they worry about long after they've left the office for the night? Their answer: the clients who *thanked* them for their hard work and who *praised* them for their victories, big and small.

Compliments are like potato chips. After you've eaten one, you have an urge for more. People tend to live up to the compliments they receive.

Heads Up

General appreciation ("Good presentation, Aaron") comes across merely as an expression of good manners. Specific appreciation ("Aaron, I was particularly impressed with the way your presentation compared...") sounds less manipulative and more believable.

Some may call it sucking up or brownnosing. Others will call it *strategic ingratiation*. Whatever you call it, stroking works. Like it or not, "kissies" are the ones who are more likely to get ahead. "It's an outgrowth of a human desire to be liked...the key to successful ingratiation is to make the person really think you like them," teaches a University of Minnesota psychologist.

The truth is we have trouble not liking someone who makes a fuss over us.

But there's a trap for the unwary: the "Eddie Haskell Syndrome." Appearing insincere. Remember how Eddie's "gee, you sure look pretty" bit never pulled the wool over June Cleaver's eyes? Discipline yourself to be subtle. It's okay if the other person knows he is being shined on—you'll score points because everyone likes to feel good about themselves.

3 Kissie Rules

1. If you can't sound sincere when sucking up, then don't even try.

2. Only suck up to people who are just a stone's throw up the company's organizational chart from you. Praising your immediate supervisor, when deserved, is fine. A mailroom clerk laying it on for the CEO sounds too much like the script of the Broadway musical *How to Succeed in Business Without Really Trying*.

3. Don't agree *too much* with what your boss has to say. That's not being a kissie—that's being a yes-man.

Heads Up

Silent appreciation doesn't mean much. Silent recognition isn't much use to anyone. A person will more readily accept your reasoning when you show recognition and appreciation for the things he or she says and does.

Consent Zone Alert

Because there are 6 common mistakes

Zone Alert #1: *Don't complain or sulk.*

"You're unfair." "You're not reasonable." A doom-and-gloom style is discomforting. A turnoff. Remember the empowering secrets of a still center and manage the curves and glitches with grace.

Zone Alert #2: *Don't look back.*

People look back only to criticize. Your argument goal is an agreement, not an admission or apology. Zero your argument in on how something is to be done rather than on why it wasn't done that way before. Suggesting possible solutions is an *issue-management technique* that moves the focus of an argument from having to justify your complaint to your proposed remedy.

Zone Alert #3: *Avoid judging the other person's actions or thoughts.*

Judgmental words—*wrong, stupid, bad, crazy, foolhardy*—will only make a person defensive and resistant.

Zone Alert #4: Don't *ask"What is your problem?"*

This makes the other person feel inadequate or lacking. It's a rare day that someone admits they were being unreasonable.

Zone Alert #5: *Don't ask "Why cant you be reasonable?"*

This question invites conflict.

Zone Alert #6: *Dont maneuver someone into a corner by pointing out discrepancies, proving them to be a liar.*

This is an invitation to fight. Instead, go to the pros' script: "You've said A and you've said B. They are at odds with each other. How can we resolve these inconsistencies?"

Heads Up

It's in the Consent Zone where you'll bring emotions under control before they reach their flash point—before positions become polarized and before ideas become crystallized from having been vigorously defended.

Finesse Hostility

Because its just like driving your car

When driving a car, you can't go from "R" to "D" without going through "N." Here's how to shift a dialogue from "Reverse" to "Neutral" so you can "Drive" your argument home.

To avoid mouth-to-mouth combat, loop the other person into your game. Try saying:

- *"You may be right in what you are saying."* This "may be" statement is non-threatening and won't prompt any new outbursts.
- *"You are probably right."* If you are reasonably sure the other person's statement is correct, then let him know.
- *"If I were in your shoes, I think I would feel the same way."* Use this non-provoking response if there is no possibility that the other person may be right. After all, if you were his mirror image—his exact alter ego—wouldn't you *have* to feel the way he does? Don't confuse *confirming* that you understand what he has said with *agreeing* with what he has said.

Heads Up

You can stand up to hostility and aggression. But that's not getting through. Being impossible back is the norm. Finessing people who are hostile is the winner's art.

Meet Arnold, California's "Governator"

Because you may be stuck in "R"

Simply saying "I'm sorry" isn't enough. A credible apology will say more: "I'm sorry because what I did was stupid...or silly...or greedy...or mean." An apology with too many "ifs" or "may haves" won't do the job. A genuine apology will acknowledge the offense. Offer a believable explanation for why it occurred (not to be confused with an excuse) and a sincere expression of shame. It will be an apology "for the harm I caused" rather than an apology "in case I may have hurt you."

A first-class apology is conclusive and unequivocal...

Allegations about Arnold Schwarzenegger's attitude towards women and the accusation by six women that he touched them in a sexual manner without their consent prompted this apology:

> So I want to say to you, yes, that I have behaved badly sometimes. Yes, it is true that I was rowdy on movie sets

and I have done things that were not right which I thought then was playful. But now I recognize that I have offended people. And to those people that I have offended, I want to say to them I am deeply sorry about that and I apologize.

But then "The Arnold" lost ground by telling a television interviewer, "I would say most of it is not true." That the accusations were just part of "trash politics."

A first-class apology should contain a statement of what will be done to correct the wrong...

We're sorry for the disruption and the inconvenience the strike has caused. Thank you for your patience and understanding....Now it's time for us to get back to the job at hand. Delivering your packages—making good on our promises. And earning back your trust.

—United Parcel Service Ad Following the End of a
Teamster's Union Strike

But a first-class apology can also explain why the wrong can't be made right...

It was not our intention to deprive people of their rights and to cause misery, but eventually apartheid led to just that....Deep regret goes much further than just saying you are sorry. It says that if I could turn the clock back, and if I could do anything about it, I would have liked to have avoided it.

—South African President F.W. de Klerk's 1993 Apology
for His National Party's Imposition of Apartheid

Heads Up
To drive your argument forward, you may need to fess up with a genuine apology. But do it right, or don't do it at all.

Chapter Summary

Construct a Consent Zone. With the right horse for the course, resistance is minimized and receptiveness maximized. Winners are never know-it-alls or tell-it-alls. Winners set a winning climate. They're enthusiastic because enthusiasm is contagious. They show appreciation for the things the other person says and does. They manage emotions by finessing hostility and making tactical apologies.

3

Link Inside the Consent Zone

Because people buy into trust first, ideas second

Arguments presented logically won't move someone emotionally. It's not enough that what you say *sounds right*. It must also *feel right* to the other person. Feeling right is about how *you* are rather than how *things* are.

In this chapter you'll discover things feel right when one finds comfort and credibility in what you say and do— when there's trust that you're not just "selling a bill of goods."

Take a Cue from Barbra Streisand
Because she knows the magic of "hi-touch"

Pop diva Barbra Streisand had been unable to sing in public for years after forgetting her lines during one anxiety-filled performance. She was now back on stage at the Anaheim Pond.

Suspended from the ceiling a few rows in front of the stage were two mega TV monitors. Only Barbra and those of us lucky enough to be seated close to the stage were able to see the screens. What were they showing? The words to Barbra's songs, yes—but also cues to chitchat and share personal anecdotes and recollections throughout the evening.

51

Stop and think about those concerts you best recall and really loved. I'll bet they had a human force. A heart-driven connection with the audience. A *"hi-touch."* A touch that wasn't available on a CD. Barbra's notes to herself were reminders to occasionally stop singing and just be Barbra. To personalize her performance by reaching out and touching her audience.

Great entertainers know that their words impact an audience's intellect. But it's their touch that captures an audience's emotions. Your touch reflects the *organic* and *spiritual force* that makes you uniquely you. Your touch is reflected in your demeanor, energy, tone of voice, rate of speech, and gestures. Good or bad, your touch reflects what you as a person are all about.

Whether you're a singer or an argument pro, more than anything else, the magic of winning flows from your touch. Flows from how you are. Flows from how you connect.

Meet Mr. Tell-Me-More

Because he sees the really big picture

Think about the people you know who always seem to have things go their way. Why is that?

It's a story I tell often. Tom, an investment firm manager, was looking for a college student to work for him during summer vacation. My son Steve was looking for summer employment in finance. The match was made.

"You know, Bob," Tom told me, "Steve is coming here to learn about things like index arbitrage and option contracts. But you and I both know that learning about those things is not nearly as important as the *real* lesson that can be learned here. All of my people are bright, industrious, capable, and well informed. Yet, somehow, a handful of them are making fortunes while others are just surviving. If Steve can understand why that is, then this will be the most valuable summer of his life."

We all know people like Tom's *survivors*—people who are talented, personable, and reasonably successful at what they attempt. We also know other people who, although neither more talented nor more personable, always seem to make things happen. They are the power people, deal doers—the *winners.*

More often than not, the big difference between the winners, the survivors, and the losers is the way they interact with other people.

As I was telling the story about Steve at a Santa Monica bookstore, a greying, middle-aged man wearing a brown tweed sport coat, muted paisley tie, and sturdy wing tips loudly whispered from the front row, "Tell me more. Tell me more. Tell me more."

Mr. Tell-Me-More, you'll soon learn more about how your style—your touch—far outweighs both your IQ and your technical proficiency. Not just in your ability to win arguments, but in everything you do. About how a more effective personal style can be had by anyone who is willing to take pause from the hurry-scurry of their day to try a more effective way.

Heads Up

Sounding right is a cognitive thing. A logic thing. Feeling right is a people thing. A connecting, linking-up emotional thing.

Whether your argument is meant for many or only one, your touch—how you link with others—will impact and influence far more than the words you write, or say...or sing.

You're Always Both—the Messenger and the Message

Because content is totality

It was such a sizzling story that Court TV wanted to televise the battle between two men I will call "George" and "Harry."

The community knew that our client George was a church leader, a successful physician, and a family man who was very much adored by his wife and teenage children. What wasn't known was that George was gay and had been leading a secret double life with Harry, his male lover. After a year, George told Harry he wanted to call it quits. Harry responded by threatening to tell all. To ensure Harry's silence, George unwillingly supported Harry's extravagant lifestyle. At the end of six years, George couldn't take it any longer and finally said "enough is enough."

Harry sued, alleging George had promised to support him forever. He argued to the jury that George's gifts to him were gifts of love—freely and willingly given.

Who was to be believed? It was touch and go, and the jury could have easily gone either way. But after six days of trial, the jury found in favor of George. Afterwards, some of the jurors were asked how they came to their unanimous decision. Was it our lawyers' arguments? The credibility of our witnesses? A blunder by our opponent's legal team?

The jurors acknowledged it was a tough call. But one dynamic played a key role in their deliberation. When Harry's apartment landlord and other witnesses came forward to testify about how they perceived the relationship, George raised his hand and motioned his wife and children to leave the courtroom. That gesture of sensitivity, of caring, of cocooning his family was George's way, his style, and it gave George a special credibility that made all the difference in the world.

Here's what I learned from a battered briefcase...

I spent three days interviewing young lawyers for our firm. Each one looked very much the part. Their personalities differed, but then you don't know what someone is really like until he's working with you.

Daniel stood out in my mind. All because of his briefcase.

Like the others, Daniel was well groomed and well dressed. A car buff would say he was "detailed to the max." His tan briefcase, however, was battered. Scarred from years of hard service. It was at odds with his shiny shoes and freshly pressed pinstripe. Curiosity got the best of me. Throwing interview protocol to the winds, I asked about the briefcase.

Daniel's father, a lawyer, died a few years before. It was his dad's briefcase. Suddenly, that beat-up old case projected an image of sensitivity and compassion. For Daniel, it was more important to carry that special case than to concern himself with what I might have thought had I not asked. Daniel's briefcase was a clear signal of what he as a person was about.

I attended a political fundraiser. One of the speakers was J.L., a well-dressed woman wearing an expensive suit with a mink-trimmed collar. The buzz in the audience was about how the speaker could be so insensitive to the feelings of animal rights advocates.

George's courtroom gesture; a battered briefcase; a mink collar. Each was a message: content is a totality. For some, J.L.'s mink collar eclipsed the words she had to say. How would you have felt about Daniel? About George?

One day you may be asked to present your argument in a talk. Here's how to save yourself a lot of aggravation and effort. Mail a copy of your speech to each person who will come to hear you. Speeches are a pain for them, too. You'll be rescuing those folks from the hassle of fighting traffic, fighting parking, and fighting for leg room. Rescued from being pulled away from things they'd rather be doing. Certainly they'll be more relaxed and better able to concentrate if they're able to peruse your words on a laid-back Sunday morning while munching on a bagel and sipping caffe latte.

But then maybe it's not such a great idea to scrap your talk. There's a persuasive advantage to connecting "live and in person."

According to the *New York Times*, reporting the results of a Roper Poll, "More than half of all Americans trust 'all' or 'most' of what local newscasters say, while less than a third have that much faith in newspaper reporters. That trust attaches to the faces on the screens, not to the stations or the backstage news directors."

Heads Up

You're more than a walkin', talkin' word-delivery system. It's you—living, breathing you—that your audience of one or many is interested in. When you're "live and in person," you have an opportunity to connect with your whole being. To be hi-touch. To be organic. To show what you as a person are all about. To create comfort, credibility, and trust so things feel right.

Take a Cue from Johnny Carson
Because he was a chameleon

It's that familiar feeling of no escape. Maybe it was a neighborhood mom peddling Girl Scout cookies for her daughter. Or a coworker hawking raffle tickets to raise money for school band uniforms. So what if you were dieting or suffering an acute budget crunch? It's easy to say No to a cause that's not your own. But it's almost impossible to say No to someone you *like*.

I made a terrible discovery when I was in 5th grade.

Some of my classmates were just plain popular. They were naturals. It was as if they'd been blessed with a super-likeability chromosome. Everything seemed to revolve around these naturally charismatic kids. That's probably why we called them "wheels." Wheels knew they had a *likeable* way. It's why year after year they had the guts to run for student office—and why year after year the rest of us voted for them.

Mine was a terrible discovery: I knew I wasn't one of the naturals—a wheel.

Maybe you aren't a natural. Few are. Maybe you aren't the "people person" you aspire to be. Or maybe you're on the quiet side. Try too hard to be likeable and you probably won't be.

My wife, Bev, is a through-and-through people person. Genuinely friendly. Naturally outgoing. A people magnet who has nothing to sell. Who isn't networking. And who isn't trying to climb a social ladder. At a social function she immediately plugs in by introducing herself to strangers. Me? I'll still be looking for the socket—a familiar face in the crowd.

Through the years, I've made another, more heartening discovery: Much of what Bev and the naturals have going for them can be adopted and put into action by anyone who is willing to change. That, with some effort, the hi-touch way super-likeable people connect can become a part of what you do. And, to a real extent, become part of who you are.

The fact that I'm not an effortless natural doesn't mean I can't adopt Bev's hi-touch style. I'm a swan. To an observer on the scene, I glide about quite gracefully. But hidden below the surface—and unlike Bev's effortless ways—there's a whole lot of paddling going on.

As the longtime host of *The Tonight Show*, Johnny Carson was warm, charming, and hospitable. Off-camera he was different. Distant. Aloof. "He really is two different people: one is the guy we all saw, and the other is the private person who becomes more private all the time," observed the former chairman of NBC.

Charisma is derived from the Greek word *kharisma*. Its root, *kharis*, means "grace." On camera, Carson had *situational charisma*. A special grace that seduced us into staying up to watch his banter with guests instead of sleeping. A charisma tailored to a specific time and setting.

Heads Up

Winning arguments is as much about style as about substance. You can develop a *situational style*. To forge a comfort connection in settings that call for it.

Meet Greg, My Comedy Workshop Instructor
Because making things feel right is an interactive process

Sometimes I just have to do something daring. At least daring for me. I'm too much of a coward for bungee jumping or skydiving. Enrolling in a stand-up comedy workshop not only fit the "daring" bill, it gave me a chance to discover new ways to make my own workshops even more student-friendly. Greg was our comedian instructor.

In a class Greg himself took, he and most of his classmates weren't African-American. Nonetheless, the class instructor arranged for his students to take lessons in—are you ready for this—African dancing!

A live band played traditional African music. Drummers deftly slapped the djembe and junjun drums. The music had an ever-changing rhythm and beat. No matter how hard Greg tried, no matter how much he counted to himself, his movements were awkward. Clumsy. In music-speak, Greg couldn't "catch the groove." Sensing Greg's frustration, the band's leader clued him into what African dancing was all about: connecting by feeling the drums…moving with the rhythm of the drums…experiencing the drums. By internalizing the beat of the drums, Greg soon found within himself the rhythm and beat that had eluded him.

In a later lesson, Greg was invited to try his hand at drumming. Even though he was no stranger to drums, Greg found drumming equally frustrating. No matter how hard he tried, he couldn't fall into sync with the other three drummers, who kept changing their tempo—going faster and faster, slowing down only to speed up again...but for no apparent reason. Again, the leader clued Greg in: the band's drummers were connecting by watching and following the lead dancers.

There are two things I haven't yet shared with you:

1. The class Greg was taking was in neuro-linguistic programming…pretty heavy stuff.
2. What Greg learned in a serious behavioral class was equally relevant in a comedy workshop.

It's also equally relevant to the art of argument. The dancers were connecting with and tracking the drummers. The drummers were connecting with and tracking the dancers. Each was leading, and each was following. Each was affecting, and each was being affected.

Heads Up

Arguing is seeking change. Change in the way the other person thinks, or feels, or sees things. Change is a process. Sometimes fast. Sometimes slow. Always affecting. Always being affected.

Meet Nike, the Shoe People

Because things feel right when you show concern

Sal T. was a client in my early days of practice. I asked Sal for a $5,000 fee advance. "Bob," he said, "just so you'll know that you never have to worry about me paying you, here's a check for $10,000." All these many years later, no other client has ever offered twice the requested advance.

We lawyers seldom ask a prospective client for information about his or her ability to pay beyond the initial advance. It's not until bills mount that we suddenly concern ourselves with the client's willingness—or ability—to pay the freight.

Sal racked up thousands of dollars in legal fees. As you have probably already guessed, he never paid another dime. I later learned that Sal had gotten undeserved credit from his landlord, printer, and others. Each of us got deposits in excess of what we requested. Sal's A+ creditworthiness came from his seeming *concern*. Concern evidenced by an overly sufficient deposit.

"To speak to a health professional, press 6"...

You've already found this out for yourself: Many of today's managed care doctors are juggling patients at an assembly-line pace. The frantic cadence is being set by efficiency minded health plan administrators. Physician–patient interpersonal skills are going the way of the doctor's house call. There is no lessening of physicians' technical expertise, but patients feel less of a sense of well-being when doctor–patient interaction is sacrificed to bottom-line profits.

Bayer Pharmaceuticals to the rescue. The aspirin folks presented physicians workshops that featured a new model for doctor–patient connecting: show concern by really listening to the patient's story before launching into the traditional medical Q&A.

Students in the School of Medicine at UCLA are coached not to listen to their patients while standing or sitting at the foot of their beds when making their hospital rounds. Concern is shown by sitting near the patient's head.

To launch its skateboarding shoe, Nike aired award-winning TV commercials. Nike's "we're concerned about skateboarders" TV pitch: "What if we treated all athletes the way we treat skateboarders?"

In skateboard's infancy, Nike seemingly wasn't concerned about the sport or about the needs of skateboarders. Skateboarders felt that Nike was ultra-uncool—arriving on the scene just in time to cash in on skateboarding's success.

A group of skateboard manufacturers rallied in support of its customers by leading a boycott against Nike. Their Johnny-come-lately battle cry: "Where was Nike when skaters were fighting to legalize our sport?" Old animosities have been forgotten, but when it counted, Nike wasn't concerned about skateboarding. When first introduced, the Nike shoe died on the shelves.

Here's what an investigative reporter pretending to be a car buyer reports:

> Customers are made to feel that the sales manager is a harsh master who would rather guzzle gasoline than sell a car for anything less than full value. Conversely, the salesmen play the role of the consumer's pal. Why, they'd give the car away if only that ogre of a sales manager would let them.

Does it sound manipulative? Maybe. But a show of *concern* works like a charm.

The 75/25 Partnering Secret

Here's a powerful trust-building secret: Listen, rather than talk, for at least 75 percent of your conversation. That's it—the whole secret. The secret works wonders because you seemed concerned enough to hear the other person out. Concerned enough to want to be partners in a dialogue. Concerned enough to want to talk *with* rather than talk *at*.

Heads Up

Things feel right when you show concern. Concern about the other person's feelings and thoughts. Concern shown by talking less and listening more. From not summarily rejecting the other person's ideas. From testing those ideas to see if they can be improved upon to emerge as real possibilities.

Meet the Kinko's Guy

Because he lets others discover his human condition

Yesterday we revered the reserved. Our heroes were stoic. Aloof. Unshakable and cool. Think John Wayne, Clint Eastwood, Humphrey Bogart. A Berkeley professor who studies the language of politics reports that 50 years ago we wanted our presidents to sound "highbrow and maybe even a little better than us, but those expectations have changed."

Today's culture embraces humility and vulnerability. A likeability that comes from an aura of approachability, concern, and understanding. Think Elvis, JFK Jr., Ronald Reagan, Princess Diana.

At John F. Kennedy Jr.'s funeral, his uncle Senator Edward Kennedy told mourners that his nephew had "amazing grace." John Jr. always introduced himself rather than assuming others knew he was the Son of Camelot. The charisma of which his uncle spoke was in being an uncommon man with a common touch.

It was no longer a secret: Prince Charles was having an affair with Camilla Parker Bowles. When the editor of *Harper's Bazaar* complimented Princess Diana on a pair of Chanel shoes she was wearing with the Chanel insignia of interlocking Cs, Di dryly let her human condition shine through: "I think of them as Charles and Camilla."

When Princess Diana died, Prince Charles was publicly chastised for not publicly putting his arms around his sons. A British journalist spoke of Charles's "emotional illiteracy."

Politicians who once sought opportunities to kiss babies are connecting in ways that show us they know how to weep and hug as well. The new art is showing just how much you care and feel.

In a presidential election debate, Ronald Reagan responded to charges that he was too out of touch and too old to be running for office. His graceful response was self-deprecation: "I will not make age an issue in this campaign. I'm not going to exploit for political purposes my opponent's youth and inexperience."

Grace is having a self-deprecating sense of humor. After being seriously wounded by would-be assassin John Hinckley, Jr. in 1981, Ronald Reagan's response to his wife, Nancy, was, "Honey, I forgot to duck." Shortly after that attempt on his life, President Reagan's approval ratings reached 90 percent, the highest on record.

A year later, the country was recovering from an economic recession, and Reagan's poll ratings plummeted. Reagan asked his pollster, "What do the figures look like?"

"Well, they're pretty bad, Mr. President."

"How bad are they?"

"Well, they're as low as they can get. They're about 32 percent."

Reagan's face lit up and he smiled. "Don't worry. I'll just go out there and try to get shot again."

California's "governator" told Silicon Valley executives that "98 percent of the second graders in California cannot read or spell simple words like Schwarzenegger. What's going on here? It's terrible."

At a travel industry association meeting Schwarzenegger asked, "And I don't know if many of you remember back in those days when I was still an award-winning actor. All right. An actor. All right, I was in the movies, okay?"

And letting his "Arnoldness" shine through, he still calls himself the governor of "Collie-for-nia."

Look who else is willing to let the world know that they, too, are just as human as the rest of us…

The "biggest surprise" of Oscar night was *Braveheart* winning five Oscars, including those for Best Picture and Best Director. The film *Braveheart* was both directed and produced by Mel Gibson, who has a "self-effacing personality…and it would be a mistake to underestimate the importance of that as a factor in the final voting," reported the *Los Angeles Times*.

Jack Chrysler is the grandson of Walter Chrysler, founder of the car company bearing his name. Needless to say, Jack, my client, has various business interests and isn't hurting. Jack's favorite is The Hitchin' Post, his Colorado country-western restaurant where there's plenty of boot-scootin' line dancing. Few customers realize that their DJ is Jack Chrysler of the Chrysler Chryslers. For fun, Jack will do private party DJ gigs in Hitchin' Post customers' backyards. Jack's fee for a private party generally ranges between $100 and $150.

And while we're on the subject of music…

My friend David Crosby of Crosby, Stills and Nash fame was appearing in concert in Los Angeles. After his second song, the rock legend paused to hike up his pants, which had slowly started to slip south. David sheepishly smiled and confessed to the audience that he was breaking a promise to his wife—that at this special concert he wouldn't "tug his pants up" on stage. "I'm sorry, Jan," he apologized. "But honey, I just had to." We love vulnerability. The audience laughed and showed David their affection with rousing applause.

John Mauceri, conductor of the Hollywood Bowl Orchestra, charms summertime audiences with stories, jokes, and tidbits about family and friends. After one concert, a woman asked John's wife, Betty, "Is your husband as charming at home as he was tonight?"

Betty replied, "I guess you've never been married!"

There's a little bit of situational charisma in all of us. This self-deprecating story was shared by the maestro himself as he reached out to us, his devoted audience.

Really. This is why Kinko's is called Kinko's. Paul Orfalea has tight curly red hair. You would have to say, *kinky* red hair. Paul is the self-deprecating founder of Kinko's and is now its Chairperson Emeritus.

Heads Up

Loosen up. We're all chronically human. We all have human shortcomings. Your way is credible and comfortable when you're not shy about showing yours.

Meet the Baskin-Robbins Ice Cream Man

Because you'll be surprised to learn his favorite flavor

Bob Hudecek was the president of Baskin-Robbins for 16 years. Bob told me there was one question he was, and still is, repeatedly asked. I'll bet it's the same question you'd ask Bob if you ever met him: "What is your favorite ice cream flavor?"

Bob always answers with a question of his own: "What's yours?" No matter what flavor you choose, Bob replies, "Mine too!" By asking a question instead of responding with his personal favorite, Bob quickly connects in a way that makes you feel glad you met him.

Oh, Bob's personal favorite? To this day, whenever I ask, he smiles and says, "You know, it's the same as yours."

Recall a social gathering you recently attended. Which stranger did you find the most interesting? Was it the one who showed an interest in you, your family, your work?

Okay, you have interesting things to say. But are they interesting to you or interesting to others? Link by talking to people about the things that *they* find important. Things that interest *them*.

How to talk to people about anything...

Super salespeople are trained to spot I'm-interested-in-what-you're-interested-in bonding clues: a shirt with a golf club logo, a cap with the name of a team, a camper parked in the driveway rather than a sedan. Expand your interests and you'll bond more easily with others. Find out what's hot—movies, books, plays. And what if you aren't knowledgeable about the things the other person is into? Asking questions is listening *and* interacting.

Mary Kay Ash believed that cosmetics could be sold at home beauty shows to small groups of women looking to improve their image. Few dreamed Mary Kay would eventually be grossing more than $200 million a year. Her success was in large part attributable to one of her hi-touch rules: "Take time to make the other person feel important."

Living-room Tupperware parties—housewives sponsoring sales parties and reaching out to other housewives—were very much a part of the American scene not too long ago. Women didn't go to Tupperware parties to learn of recent advances in rolling-pin technology or pasta storage options. Nor did they go to hear lettuce-saver lids being "burped" to remove excess air, "the mortal enemy of freshness." The carefully choreographed parties included other-centric games that gave women a feeling of self-worth and a sense of female solidarity that "they weren't likely to find elsewhere," reported *Newsweek*.

IN THE NEIGHBORHOOD...

Pretend you live in a quiet middle-class neighborhood. Children play on sidewalks. Family pets roam from yard to yard. Three blocks away on Elm Street is a scattering of small businesses. Theater Corp. U.S.A. wants to build a six-screen multiplex theater there. You feel this would be a major tragedy. To your surprise, many neighbors are ambivalent. Some even look forward to being able to walk to the movies. You'll be arguing for your neighbors to unite in protest against the multiplex being built. You'll be arguing with the city and Theater Corp. that a multiplex doesn't belong on Elm Street.

We'll come back to your argument as you discover the steps of having a winning argument...

Power linking is affecting and being affected. Allowing your ideas to be tested by fair and logical examination. Acknowledging that you understand a critical comment, but not taking the criticism personally. Here's a great way to discipline yourself to be other-centric: Imagine you're building *Question Sandwiches*. Set each of your questions between two generous slices of silence.

Heads Up

Make things feel right by being seemingly other-centric. Comfort and credibility come from serving Question Sandwiches to show that the other person's answer is important to you.

Meet an Infomercial Producer

Because things feel right when feelings are shared

We need people who can create empathy. People who can say, I was just like you. I've been where you've been. I was overweight. I was poor. I had problems with my hair. I had problems with my skin.

—Infomercial Producer Being Interviewed on
60 Minutes

Fans will say just about anything to get their hands on a favorite author's newest book before it hits Barnes & Noble or Borders. An editor at a large publishing house told me about the frantic telephone call she got from a woman who knew the power of empathy: "My father's in the hospital dying. Could you get the book to me now so he can read it before he goes?" The editor felt compelled to FedEx the printed, but not yet distributed novel. Was the woman's story true? The editor says she never really knew.

A banner flown from an airplane over an Illinois–Northwestern football game in Evanston, Illinois, somehow seemed to say it all about the then First Lady and her alleged involvement in the Whitewater scandal:

Hillary: You have the right to remain silent.

But when Hillary Clinton was later humiliated by the Monica Lewinsky scandal, she became the recipient of a national outpouring of empathy that pushed her favorable rating to an all-time high in the polls and helped get her elected to a Senate seat.

 BACK IN THE NEIGHBORHOOD...

"I know you feel that it would be nice for our kids to be able to walk to the movies. And there's no denying that a movie theater is a place where our kids could connect with friends on Saturday afternoons. And I know you share with me an awareness of the problems a multiplex brings with it. My hope is that you're considering the minuses as well as the pluses."

Heads Up

Can you ever build a feeling of togetherness without a chatty phone call or an in-person visit?

Shared feelings. A sense of emotional kinship. Few things have greater power to forge a "feels right" bond. To win assent.

How to Get Your Husband to Shed 40 Pounds

Because things feel right when power is seemingly shared

Quick Quiz

Your husband needs to shed 40 pounds. You have gone through the suggest-you-lose-weight phase and the nagging-and-harping phase. Now, which of the following is the most compelling thing you can say?

A. "How are you ever going to lose 40 pounds?"

B. "You must exercise more and eat less."

C. "How can you lose 40 pounds and have fun doing it?"

D. "Dear, when you're naked, you look like the letter Q."

The quiz answer coming up soon. But first...

Almost a million boxes of Jell-O are sold every day. We're devoted to Jell-O, especially red, the flavor we hold most dear. The ease of making Jell-O was emphasized in a Norman Rockwell ad showing a little girl unmolding Jell-O for her doll. From its very first ads in 1904, Jell-O *empowered* homemakers to turn out a can't-fail dessert: "How often is some ingredient forgotten and not rightly proportioned, and the dessert spoiled? This will never occur if you use Jell-O."

Even a parking space can be empowering. Bingo! You have staked out your space. The car that's there now has its reverse lights lit—a sign that the parking space's present occupant is poised to pull out. You're at the ready. The guy in the space knows you're waiting—but he isn't moving. What gives? He's just sitting there, checking out his face in the rearview mirror, messing around with his hair, adjusting his sunglasses.

A study of parking lot behavior took place at an Atlanta-area mall. On average, it takes drivers almost twice as long to back out of a parking space knowing another car is waiting for their spot. Having control over a parking space is empowering. When the space is turned over, empowerment is relinquished.

Forbes magazine calls itself "the capitalist tool." A letter in my morning mail read: "It's my pleasure to offer you an extraordinary financial tool...." Tools by their very nature are empowering devices. What tool was the letter pitching? A Visa card.

As for the husband with a weight problem, the answer is C. With choices A, B, and D, your spouse will feel depressed and defensive. With choice C, he is likely to come up with his own answers as to how he'll shed the weight. Choice C's question is empowering.

Heads Up

Create an aura of *interactive power*. What you say feels right when power is seemingly shared. Shared power is comfortable. Your position versus the other person's position is a struggle to have power *over* rather than power *with*.

Meet the Former "Duchess of Pork"
Because unless things feel right, who cares what you say

"Meet the real exotic dancer behind tonight's movie...the news at 11!"

Local TV news lost most of its credibility with me long ago. I'm no longer coaxed to stay up by shameless tie-ins masquerading as news. Suckered by promos that promised much more than they ever delivered.

In Chapter 5 you'll discover how to make your *logic* credible so things *sound right*. But here's how to make *yourself* more credible so things *feel right*.

Awhile back, I was lucky enough to take travel-writing classes from Jack Adler, one of the best travel writers in the business. Jack's mantra was "credibility, credibility, credibility."

And Jack taught us how to be credible. "Stay away from 'gee whiz' reporting." Superlatives can rarely be supported," he cautioned. Avoid over-statements and absolutes such as *never, always, great,* or *best*. Absolutes have a certainty and finality that are seldom true.

The defrocked Duchess of York—fresh from a divorce, notorious for tanning topless and having her toes sucked by her financial advisor—was paid $1.7 million to be a pitchwoman for Weight Watchers. Why Fergie? Once nick-named "The Duchess of Pork," Fergie "represents honesty," a marketing consultant told a national periodical. A sample "honesty confession" from the Duchess: "Last weekend I was quite naughty. It was sausage rolls again. Sausages wrapped in phyllo pastry, cooked with fat in the oven. Yum!"

Credibility can be easily lost...

Reader Alert: If you're a Bausch & Lomb contact lens customer, then you may want to be sitting down when you read this.

Bausch & Lomb formerly sold its contact lenses under three different names. Optima FW lenses, the most expensive, were advertised to be used for one year. Medalist, the next most expensive, were advertised to be used for up to three months. SeeQuence 2, the least expensive, were advertised to be used for up to two weeks. The price difference among the three Bausch & Lomb names was significant.

Contact lens wearers like Bausch & Lomb lenses. They expect them to be high in quality. They also expect that Bausch & Lomb will make a profit—small or large—from the sale of those lenses.

Now here's what lens wearers never expected: All three brands of lenses were absolutely identical! Only their names and prices differed.

State investigators in 17 states claimed the whole scenario was a scam. Bausch & Lomb said the branding was nothing more than a clever marketing strategy and denied any wrongdoing.

The lenses Bausch & Lomb makes are a fine product. But the company shattered its credibility by violating consumer expectations.

How credible will Philip Morris be in the future when it makes claims about "light" low-tar cigarettes, improved filters, or reduced smoking risk after knowing that...

Philip Morris had information that confirmed smoking health risks as early as 1953, but told the public that "authorities" have "reached no agreement" on what causes lung cancer. That there is "no proof" that smoking causes cancer and that smoking is "not injurious to health." They launched a public disinformation campaign to counter mounting scientific evidence about the strong correlation between smoking and serious illness. This campaign manipulated the mass media to suppress or make light of adverse new and scientific studies.

As pressure mounted, Philip Morris announced the creation of a "research institute" dedicated to finding the "truth." Philip Morris never intended to keep its word. The institute was permitted to conduct very little research, and those results confirming the deadly link were hidden at a secret lab in Germany.

But lost credibility can be restored...

Forget about full-page color glossies of smiling flight attendants. Forget about the stats on its newest jumbo jets. Forget about the "friendly skies" hype. Awhile back, United Airlines wanted its stockholders to know that its primary concern is how passengers feel about their airline. Building on a we-are-learning-from-our-past theme, a United Annual Report let it all hang out by printing actual passenger complaints and vowing to do better.

A sample gripe printed in the report: A passenger commenting on Shuttle by United wrote that it "provides treatment akin to that of Trailways, Greyhound, or the worst of the bargain-basement airlines."

After reading unvarnished comments like that, you're apt to find United's promises of improvement more believable.

Do you remember this television commercial: "You tried electric. You hated it. Years ago, the whole thing just didn't feel right. This time it will. First of all, this isn't the same Norelco your father used."

Were you convinced Norelco was doing things differently? I was.

Nike's overseas labor practices were being publicly criticized—sweatshop conditions, meager wages. Former UN Ambassador Andrew Young was hired by Nike to look into the allegations. After visiting 12 Asian factories and interviewing hundreds of workers, Young concluded: "Nike is doing a good job...but Nike can and should do better."

Nike's we're-on-the-right-track response appeared in national advertisements: "Nike agrees. Good isn't good enough in anything we do. We can and will do better."

Heads Up

Create an aura of credibility. If others already have positive expectations about you, don't disappoint them the way Bausch & Lomb and Philip Morris did.

Chapter Summary

The other fellow will buy into your argument when it both *feels right* and *sounds right*. Things feel right when there is a climate of credibility, comfort, and trust.

When you argue, you're seeking change. Change means movement. Movement means friction. As things begin to feel right, friction fades and a link-to-lead bond emerges.

CHAPTER

4

Lead Inside the Consent Zone

Because you dont push, you lead

Arguments are won by having control over how you will be (see Chapter 1). By creating a Consent Zone before linking (see Chapter 2). By linking before leading (see Chapter 3). And by leading (See Chapter 4) before making your logic argument (see Chapter 5).

In this chapter you'll discover how to lead the other person to your desired outcome.

Meet Lisa, One of Our Staffers

Because if you can't get her interested, you're going nowhere

Lisa, a member of our law office staff, is bright and well-informed. She clearly understands the health risks of smoking. Unfortunately, she has a "belief" of her own: life is to be enjoyed and no one lives forever. If she didn't smoke, she would be a nervous wreck. She would gain weight. Smoking is bad for you, but then so are a million other things.

Who attends pro-life rallies? The answer is pro-life advocates. Who listens to pro-choice speeches? Pro-choice advocates. Who turns out to

71

hear Republicans? Republicans turn out to hear Republicans. Democrats do the same for their candidates. Who really reads advertisements? The answer: people who have *already bought* the truck, or diet program, or personal computer being pitched.

The task of using reason to influence Lisa and others who don't already agree with you may well be an uphill battle.

How do you get people to give fat grams a second thought? By changing what they believe so they'll *want* to become actively involved in their own healthcare.

How do you get people to start recycling? Start caring about endangered species? Stop polluting? By changing what they believe so they'll *want* to be partners in saving our environment.

How do you get apathetic people to care about the downside of a neighborhood multiplex? By changing what they believe will happen if it's built.

People are interested in what you have to say when you show them there's something in it for them. As the story goes, a dog lover invented a new dog food. He sold his invention to one of the country's biggest dog food companies. They created a fancy package, found a mascot, and spent millions of dollars marketing the new product. But the dog food didn't sell. The marketing plan was again analyzed, but failed to explain why the dog food sat on grocers' shelves. Finally, a member of the marketing team solved the mystery: "Maybe dogs don't like our product."

Your argument can be "well-packaged" and delivered with passion, but it isn't going to "sell" unless there's something in it that the other guy likes.

Heads Up

People aren't influenced by what you tell them. They're influenced by what they hear. Don't confuse motion with progress. Keep it simple. Keep it relevant. And keep it interesting by showing the other fellow what's in it for him.

Meet Debra, the Matchmaker
Because people judge things by comparing

Debra, who owns a successful matchmaking service, has this advice for her staff: "If you tell a woman she'll be meeting a guy who has a 'great personality and is really a hunk,' she'll be sadly disappointed if anybody short of Brad Pitt knocks at her door. But if you say her date is 'personable and has a nice appearance,' she won't be disappointed when she meets the not-so-hunky and not-so-charming Joe Average."

During a class for Beverly Hills real estate brokers, a high-earning superstar shared the logic of her success: "Show the overpriced fixer-upper first. Later, when I take my prospects to a fairly priced home in good condition, they'll feel like they've discovered a real bargain."

Another broker told the class that she uses the same logic in reverse: "I tell prospects, 'The place I'm going to show you needs some work, but with a little imagination and effort it may fit your needs.' I then drive them to a well-maintained home in their price range. Expecting the worst, the house comes across like the Palace of Versailles."

Model home interior decorators are also masters of this *contrast tactic*. Here's the advice a decorator gave my home-builder client: "If a regular-size bed will make a model bedroom look cramped, furnish the room with a crib. If the master bedroom will look skimpy with a queen or king-size bed, furnish it with a double bed."

A tram takes visitors on the Universal Studios Tour in Hollywood through the back lot. That's where the studio stores its facades of stores, houses, and buildings. Mike, our tram guide, pointed out that the buildings had front doors of varying heights. To make larger actresses appear petite, the scene would be shot in front of a facade with an oversize door. To make a small actor appear larger, the shoot would be in front of a facade with a shorter-than-normal door.

Quick Quiz

You are an Olympic Games contender. There's slim chance you'll win a gold medal. But the chances are pretty good that you'll go home with a silver or a bronze. Will you be happier with a silver medal or with a bronze medal?

Read on for the answer...

A survey of 2004 Athens Olympians revealed that silver medalists weren't as happy with their medals as were those who won bronze. Why? Because second-place winners regretted not having garnered gold. The third-place finishers were happy to have even won a coveted medal.

Pretend you've been given the news that a wealthy cousin you never met left you and other distant relatives $10,000 each. You're thrilled and excited. The next week, you learn that the amount bequeathed to those other equally distant relatives was really $50,000. Upon learning this, will you still be as happy about being left $10,000? Probably not. Happiness comes from the comparisons we make: what we have, what we expect, what we want, and what we think we deserve.

A local charity has as its annual fund-raiser a private screening of a soon-to-be-released movie, followed by supper. The tab for the "flick'n food" is $150. Everyone knows the movie will be in general citywide distribution within a week or so of the private screening.

Here's the reasoning behind this fund-raising tactic: Charities have limited success prying loose donations when there is no corresponding donor benefit. Friends and acquaintances who receive invitations to attend the $150 screening have some wiggle room because they can decline by checking a box that reads, "Sorry, I can't attend, but my $50 donation is enclosed."

It's like magic. Suddenly the mail is filled with $50 donations without a corresponding tangible benefit. Why? Fifty bucks is a lot of money, but compared to shelling out $150 for a movie and a not-so-great dinner, it's the deal *du jour*.

Argument pros know to seek more than they expect to receive:

"Will you chaperon Scout Camp the third *week* of January?"

"No way!"

"Well, then, how about chaperoning the snow *weekend* in October?"

"Well, I guess so."

As the local charity and the scout leader backed down from their big requests ($150 for the screening and dinner; a whole week of chaperoning), they made smaller requests (a $50 donation; a weekend in the snow). Those smaller requests were their concessions. Concessions that are gladly grabbed up by writing a check for $50 and agreeing to a few days judging snowman-building contests.

Think back to the last time you went car shopping. Does this sound all too familiar? It's how a Honda dealer coaches its salespeople:

Lesson 1: The customer needs entry-level two-door wheels. Show the Accord before you show the Civic. The Accord sells for about $4,000 more than a Civic. The Civic's sticker shock is softened when the prospect hears the Accord's price.

Lesson 2: The Civic comes in three models (least expensive, medium price, and luxury). If the salesperson shows the least expensive model first, the medium-price model appears expensive. If the luxury model is shown first, by comparison the medium-price model seems suddenly affordable.

Lesson 3: Hold off pitching options (fancier wheels, sound and security systems) until the basic deal has been cast. Once the customer has agreed to shell out close to 20 grand, what's another $1,500 or so?

 ## BACK IN THE NEIGHBORHOOD...

"We have choices. 1. We can do nothing and enjoy having movies so close to home. 2. We can consent if traffic can be controlled and security is assured. 3. We can say No to the multiplex."

Quick Quiz

You are sitting down to watch TV with a bag of M&Ms. Will you eat more M&Ms if you're holding a 2-pound bag than if you're holding a 1-pound bag?

Read on for the answer...

In a University of Illinois study, the average number of M&Ms consumed by those holding the 1-pound bag was 112. For those holding a 2-pound bag, it was 156. A sweet reminder that everything is relative.

And if you want to look young and thin, just hang out with old, fat people...

Tip

People judge things by comparing them. Want to win approval for your idea? Create choices. Make your argument's desired outcome the most attractive choice you present.

---

4 Ways to Add Credibility to Your Argument

Because it's not enough that you're credible—what you say has to appear credible

1. There's Credibility in Being Precise

Here's how I coached Jake, my plumber: Make a $296.75 bid and it sounds well thought out. Deliberated. But if you bid $300, it will sound "pulled out of a hat." Cavalier. An invitation to your customer to haggle.

"Ivory soap is 99-44/100% pure." Would Ivory soap's purity be just as credible if it proclaimed, "Ivory soap is very, very pure"?

"Our 747s depart on time 95% of the time," boasts Japan Airlines. Would Japan Airline's record for being on time be as credible if it proclaimed, "Our 747s are almost always on time"?

"Clorox Clean-Up kills 99.9% of household bacteria and viruses." Would Clorox Clean-Up's germ-killing ability be as credible if it proclaimed, "Hardly any household bacteria or viruses survive when you clean with Clorox"?

The specific is more credible than the generic.

"She is consistent" is an inference. But saying, "She closes seven out of 10 sales" is a credible statement of fact.

"It was a really exciting game" is a flat, lifeless abstraction. But saying, "There were three touchdowns in the last 10 minutes" gives credibility to it being an "exciting" game.

"He is reliable" is a judgmental conclusion that doesn't convey credibility the same way as saying, "He never missed a day's work in 12 years on the job."

2. There's Credibility in "Who Else Says So"

It's a luxury not having to make difficult decisions—sifting through the pros and cons, evaluating the facts, gathering new facts, analyzing and separating, battling the forces of reason. It's easier to put our decision-making processes on autopilot. To simply pick up on what others have seen fit to do. We are influenced by the power of "who else says so."

My sister and I checked out at least a dozen managed care facilities when it became apparent that my widowed dad could no longer live safely in his own home.

It was nice to tour facilities with linen tablecloths in the dining room, fresh flowers in public areas, big-screen TVs in the recreation room, caregivers in crisp white uniforms. But the place my sister and I chose for Dad had few of these amenities.

Our facility of choice was spartan and had an antiseptic quality. During my facility tour, instead of talking about how fresh the flowers were, I was introduced to occupants who couldn't recall the name of the president of the United States or the year they were born. The facility manager proudly identified those occupants for us: the former editor of the state's largest newspaper, a former top-level exec at Bank of America, and a once prominent UCLA professor. If this facility was the choice of their caring families, then certainly it had to be our logical choice too.

Have you ever been asked to rate a movie at a pre-release sneak preview? Or maybe you were part of an audience that was polled after a film's release?

When Warner Brothers previewed the classic film *Goodfellas*, the screening scores weren't good. Audiences said they'd be reluctant to recommend the movie to a friend. Studio pros know that the pre- and post-release polling results will generally be similar. When *Goodfellas* was finally released, critics around the country hailed it as one of the great American films. Doing an about-face, moviegoers took a cue from the critics. The post-release polling scores skyrocketed, fueled by the power of who else says so. *Goodfellas* went on to get six Oscar nominations, and *Sight & Sound* named it the fourth best film of the last 25 years.

Credibility is in the eye of the beholder...

Movie ads tout reviewers' upbeat comments. All too quickly, I choose movies because of what "those in the know" have to say. I'm constantly relearning that a movie critic's thumbs-up or four stars isn't gospel. A case in point, the big-budget musical *Moulin Rouge*, starring Nicole Kidman. In its annual year-end wrap-up, *Time*'s critics declare the best and worst movies of the year. For 2001, critic Richard Corliss named *Moulin Rouge* his "Year's Best" #2 slot. That same year, *Time*'s Richard Schickel pegged the film as #1 "Year's Worst." What's credible depends on which critic you find credible.

And there is even credibility in the not so credible...

A ticker-tape parade was thrown by the city of New York for its Yankees World Series champions. The mayor's office boasted to the press that a crush of 3.5 million people had lined the mile-long parade route. The 3.5 million "statistic" became widely repeated headline news.

Weeks later, an investigative reporter set the record straight: "Even granting that the slimmest of folks showed up, they would still have to line up 1,000 deep, an impossibility on the cramped streets of lower Manhattan."

 BACK IN THE NEIGHBORHOOD...

Call upon the logic of what other people—real or imagined—are saying: *"People who have given considerable thought to the issue are very much opposed to a six-screen theater....Most people are saying to vote No."*

---

3. There's Credibility in "If I Can, You Can Too"

We are influenced when we see what people who are similar to us have accomplished. It's the logic of "if I can, you can too." Show the other guy how your idea can work for him as it has worked for you and others. The testimonial is a tried-and-true advertising technique because it works. And it also works to win arguments.

Quick Quiz

You're a TV producer planning an ab-machine infomercial. Who will best sing your product's praises: A former Mr. Universe with a washboard stomach? Or Mr. Sit-In-The-Office-All-Day who burned off 3 inches of flab with your machine?

You're selling a "Math Made Easy" course. Will your best spokesperson be the professor who developed the course? Or the high school junior who went from D's to A's in three short weeks?

Infomercial testimonials feature down-the-street kinda folks. You know, the ones who bought get-rich-fast tapes and are now excitedly holding up their "trophy check"—a memorial of having closed a no-money-down or hardly-any-money-down deal. Often they are plain-wrap folks with an every-man demeanor. Although their English is sometimes lacking, their implied message is crystal clear: "If I can do it, so can you!"

Multilevel marketing companies use "opportunity meetings" to recruit new distributors into their ranks. These meetings frequently feature a "lineup of stars"—real people who have achieved incredible success selling cosmetics, nutritional products, diet aids, or whatever.

4. There's Credibility by Appearing to Be "In the Know"

"Four out of five dentists recommend...." "Tylenol is the pain reliever used most." Do you remember these ads? Our world is just too complex for each of us to know a lot about everything. We rely on others to guide and inform us, and we put stock in what experts—real or perceived—have to say. We find it easy to believe what they believe.

"Shrinks Share Personal Details" was the title of a newspaper article about what's new among mental health professionals. What's new is a twist in how they go about relating to their patients. Professionals are now confiding things about themselves to their patients. One psychologist shares his experience as a child of divorce when treating patients with similar issues because sharing "can enhance the credibility of what the therapist is saying."

Estée Lauder wants you to believe what its sales clerks have to tell you. The makeup giant, which also owns Clinique, Origins, and Mac brands, now dominates the first floor of most department stores. Using it's-okay-to-believe-me titles, Estée Lauder calls its clerks "Beauty Advisors" and trains them to enhance their image of expertise and authority by wearing "minimum" jewelry and "neat, classic" hairstyles. Clinique clerks are "Consultants," a name that creates a dermatological image. Origins has "Guides," a name that conveys an image of "natural" and believability. Mac clerks are "Makeup Artists," a name that throws off an edgier, but still in-the-know image.

Come across as someone whose logic is to be trusted. An expert...a maven...someone who has been there, done that. Be an authority. Or at least have the aura of someone in the know.

 ## BACK IN THE NEIGHBORHOOD...

"I met with our city councilwoman, who told me that increased traffic and noise will be unavoidable. I also met with a real estate appraiser, who said that a change in the character of our neighborhood will cause our homes to be worth less."

You don't need to be in the know to appear to be in the know. Some real-life examples:

Oprah Winfrey is an expert on many topics. Mad cow disease isn't one of them. But when a food safety activist on *The Oprah Winfrey Show* suggested that mad cow disease posed a dire threat to the health of Americans who eat beef, Oprah exclaimed, "You just stopped me cold from eating another burger!" The price of cattle and cattle futures plunged the day that particular show aired, and Texas cattlemen filed suit against Winfrey. "People of influence have to be careful about what they say," cautioned the owner of the Amarillo Livestock Auction.

The whole debacle is now known among cattlemen as "the Oprah crash."

Clients will sometimes ask me to form a corporation for their new start-up businesses. I usually ask why. Is there a tax reason for being incorporated? Are the checks and balances of a corporate structure necessary? Is a corporate structure needed to shelter the principals from liability?

Sometimes the only reason a client will go to the expense and effort of incorporating is because, as my client H.K. said, "It's easier to make deals when I say I am the president of a corporation…it's a position of authority. Both my business and I take on an image of importance."

C.H. is a con man who bilked millions from clients to feed his champagne appetites for contemporary art and diamonds. "Why would you doubt him?" one of his victims asked. C.H.'s victims spoke of C.H.'s "upper-crust British accent," "impeccable clothes," "9-carat diamond ring," and "arrogance." C.H. had all the trappings and the air of authority that victims of swindlers so often cite.

A Hummer is a clunky colossus that was once called a Humvee (short for High Mobility Multipurpose Wheeled Vehicle). The Hummer was originally designed for the U.S. Army, but has since been turned loose on the civilian market. It is now the oversized Tonka toy of choice among the rich and incredibly trendy. Seven feet wide, more than 6 feet high, weighing in at 10,300 pounds, and getting 10 miles or less to a gallon of fuel, the Hummer casts an authoritarian-like presence. "Never under estimate the practical applications of intimidation," is how the Hummer brochure puts it.

Have you ever gone out to dinner with wine aficionados? You know, the folks who talk endlessly about a wine's roundness, muskiness, tannin, bouquet, and complexity. I will admit it. Sometimes I can't really tell the difference between the twist-off cap stuff and a pricey vintage offering. So what's a guy to do when he feels outgunned when it comes to having an intimate knowledge of the grape? Take a course called "How to Be a Wine Snob." And that's exactly what I did.

My taste in wine hasn't changed. But when confronted with a "what do you think of this wine?" situation, a lot of people believe I'm in the know. It's all because of the one-size-fits-all response I learned in class: With a thoughtful look, I'll nonchalantly reply, "Hmm—it's an amusing wine, but it's certainly not distinguished."

When do you feel comfortable jaywalking? Studies reveal that three-and-a-half times as many people will follow a jaywalker in a business suit crossing the street against a "DON'T WALK" sign than will follow that same jaywalker when he's dressed in a worker's shirt and pants. If he were dispensing advice, would the well-dressed fellow be more believable to you than the guy wearing a work shirt?

And while we're talking "Tie Power"…

Once a year, Ben & Jerry's ice cream stores have Customer Appreciation Day, when they give away free single cones. Instead of being presented with a single scoop like everyone else in line, I was handed a double Cherry Garcia. "Why am I getting two scoops?" I quizzed the teenage counterman. "Don't know...guess it's 'cause you're wearing a tie."

Tip

People are influenced by the thinking of those who appear to be "in the know." By the logic of "who else says so." By the logic of "if I can, you can too." By the logic of someone who has the aura and attitude of someone in the know. And sometimes by just wearing a tie!

Meet Raj, Who Telephoned Me 15 Years Later

Because stories are a powerful way to lead

Raj telephoned to say he needed a lawyer. He introduced himself by saying that 15 years earlier he attended my UCLA workshop. When we met, Raj complimented me on my negotiating-skills workshop and told me how he remembered so much of what he learned that day. Raj didn't play back my serious class remarks. Instead, he talked about the anecdotes and stories I shared with the class to get those points across.

How do you create a warmth and empathy that another person can *feel*? How do you transfer emotional energy? It's easy. Tell a story.

What could be more poignant than the dripping-with-emotion Campbell's soup TV ad where a very shy young girl and her foster mother finally bond when Mom offers the girl—you guessed it!—a bowl of Campbell's soup?

Or what could be more heart-tugging than the commercial where six children from two different families try to persuade their single parents to marry? The kids' tactic—whipping up a meal for the parents that includes Campbell's soup. The parents tell the kids—now here comes the big surprise—that in fact they just got engaged!

So why doesn't Campbell's soup just come right out and tell us Campbell's soup is "M'm! M'm! Good!"? Because people are motivated when you push their emotional buttons. As for the Campbell's soup ads: "There is an emotional connection being made that transcends being hot and delicious," says the creative chief of a national advertising agency.

Stories are among the most powerful persuasive tools ever discovered by man. Jesus used them for his teaching, and we know them as parables. They've been repeated for more than 2,000 years.

Abraham Lincoln filled his stories with a wry humor that came from his boyhood on the American frontier...

A young Abraham Lincoln was pleading a case before a jury. The circumstantial evidence was stacked against him, even though right was on his side. Lincoln persuaded the jury to ignore the logic of the circumstantial evidence by telling this story:

> A farmer back home was sitting on his front porch, when suddenly his 6-year-old son came running from the barn and said, "Father, father, the hired man is in the hayloft with big sister. The hired man is pulling down his pants and big sister is lifting up her skirt, and I fear they are going to pee on the hay."
>
> "Now, now, son," the farmer said calmly. "You have all the facts right, but you have reached the wrong conclusion."

A story is something you visualize rather than intellectualize. A story isn't something you lay on the other person. A story is something you share. It's something by which you and other people emotionally connect. A story imparts nothing to question, reject, refute. A person who is told a story has nothing to defend.

A story transfers feelings when it is crafted in human terms rather than lifeless abstractions. Your most compelling story will be drawn from your own experience—something you saw with your own eyes, something that you heard with your own ears.

A story has the capacity to clarify the obscure and simplify the complex. The best stories are the ones you tell in plain language.

Here's a personal favorite about how the plain language of a comic book story was long remembered...

The freighter *Al Kuwait*, carrying a cargo of 6,000 sheep, capsized in Kuwait's harbor in 1964. Fearing their water supply would be poisoned by the decaying sheep carcasses, local residents desperately needed to raise the ship from the harbor bottom. The critical question: How could the ship be raised?

A Danish manufacturer came to the rescue with an idea he'd gotten from—of all things—a 1949 Walt Disney comic book. He recalled the story of how a sunken yacht popped to the surface when Donald Duck and his nephews—Huey, Dewey, and Louie—stuffed Ping-Pong balls into the doomed vessel.

Kuwait's water supply was spared when the Dane injected 27 billion polystyrene balls into *Al Kuwait*'s hull and the freighter rose to the harbor surface. A triumph of engineering and a long-remembered story about the creativity of four cartoon ducks.

Your story argument should have a clearly recognizable *theme*. A self-revealing reason or truth for being told. For example, in an environmental case, a lawyer made the jury want to hear more when his story began with this theme: "This is a case about whether the government has to obey the same rules as the rest of us." In another case, a lawyer's story involving a complex banking case began with this simple, compelling theme: "They lied, they stole. We want our money back."

Heads Up

To change how the other person feels, lead with a story. Stories are compelling, memorable, and easily understood. Stories convey warmth, empathy, and—most importantly—your human spirit.

Meet a Toyota Dealer

Because he knows there's comfort in following the lead of others

You've seen how people find comfort and guidance in doing what others are doing. Being imitators saves them time and energy by validating that what they feel or think is right on.

We all know it's okay to hoot and holler at a ball game, but not in a movie theater. And we know it's okay to pick up French fries with our fingers, but not so okay to pick up string beans or asparagus the same way. Just as it's okay to drink beer right out of the can at a barbecue, but a glass is the way to go at a nicer restaurant.

Jerry Seinfeld asks, "What's the thing with tipping jars? Is it a tip for just turning around?" Takeout-counter employees who salt their tip cups with folding money are more likely to get generous tips because "other people" have demonstrated that leaving green (rather than a coin or two) is the correct and proper thing to do. And this whole let-me-show-you-the-way thing didn't start at Starbucks. Church ushers have known for years that worshipers contribute more when collection baskets are passed around with some money already in the basket.

Customers buying cars at southern California's largest Toyota dealership make their way past "closing tables" strategically placed around the showroom floor. Entering the dealership, the very first thing they see are customers buying Toyotas. The right-off-the-bat message: "This is the time and the place to make a really good buy on a new car."

Meet a "Low-Baller"
Because everyone needs to save face

People need to be consistent with themselves and with their previously announced beliefs.

Have you experienced either of the following examples?

- Dieters who announce to friends and family their commitment to shed weight are more likely to stick to their diets.
- Companies whose staffers are asked to write down their personal sales goals get better results than companies that don't seek written commitments.

Sellers of aluminum siding, time-share resorts, and other high-pressure hypesters all know the trick: customers who personally fill in sales contract blanks are less likely to kill the deal during the cooling-off period.

In 25-words-or-less "Why I love..." contests, prize seekers submit brief testimonials. These testimonials become statements of commitment. The contestant, having gone on record as liking the product, is likely to remain a customer for life.

Low-balling—deliberately throwing out a lower price than one intends to charge—is an unfair sales tactic. A car dealer's confession to an investigative reporter explains how this tactic plays out:

> We tell the customer we've discovered a "mistake" in the quoted price. A sales manager will then apologize for reneging rather than losing money on the deal. Low-balling works

because customers usually agree to the increased price because their mind-set to buy has been cast.

Call it "getting your foot in the door." Getting that small first order. A commitment—that initial order—changes a buyer's self-perception from "prospect" to "customer." With a customer's mind-set, former prospects are glad to look at samples or try other products. Doing so is consistent with being a customer. Customers have an attitude of receptiveness. People who aren't customers have an attitude of resistance.

Quick Quiz

I know. You never win anything. But pretend for the moment that in a local restaurant's drawing, you *win* a $125 special Saturday night dinner for two. The dinner must be enjoyed next Saturday night—no exceptions. Later in the week you are invited to a friend's party that same Saturday. Someone you would like to meet will be at your friend's home that evening. Will you choose to have dinner at the restaurant or go to your friend's party?

Now pretend that you *prepaid* $125 for a special Saturday night dinner for two. The $125 is nonrefundable and the day can't be changed. Later in the week you are invited to a friend's party that same Saturday. Somebody you would like to meet will be at your friend's home that evening. Will you choose to have dinner at the restaurant or go to your friend's party?

Most people are inclined to dine with their friends in the first situation and at the restaurant in the second. Why? Because to ignore money we've already spent is being *inconsistent* with ourselves.

Our need to be consistent with ourselves is also the need to act in ways that are consistent with what others expect of us. Retreating from an announced position means appearing to others as being inconsistent.

Call it the *New Revelation Tactic*. Revealing new information empowers a person to gracefully back down and save face. Peter Sellers, Inspector Clouseau of *Pink Panther* movie fame, trips in public and falls down. "I see there's nothing of interest on the floor, so I'll take a seat." Few of us can finesse embarrassment as graciously as Clouseau. Want your argument to be warmly received? Then empower the other person to sidestep from what would otherwise be the indignity of an embarrassing situation.

BACK IN THE NEIGHBORHOOD...

"I discovered something you may not be aware of about what happens when multiplex theaters are built in neighborhoods like ours..." or "Here's a surprising twist on what happens to real estate value when six-screen theaters are built...."

Do you have an about-to-be-married niece who thinks of you as being rich? If so, here's a pretty safe guess: your inclination will be to buy her a more expensive wedding gift than you would otherwise purchase.

So why do you tip? Is it for better service? If your answer is Yes, then here's a shocking fact: the relationship between the tip you leave and the future service you'll be getting is very weak, reports the *Hospitality Research Journal*. The truth is, we tip because it's expected. We act in ways that are consistent with what we believe others expect of us. And, according to University of Houston researchers, when we don't leave the expected tip, we feel embarrassment, shame, self-consciousness, and anxiety.

We love people and things whose actions are consistent with our expectations. "This is why June Cleaver never ran off with the UPS guy, why Dorothy preferred Kansas to Oz, and why Cal Ripken is a god," noted the *Washington Post*.

Did you notice? It's gone! That plug of cotton in Bayer Aspirin bottles. For years, cotton was the bottle's immobilizer—it kept the tablets from joggling around and breaking up. But since the 1980s, cotton really hasn't been necessary. That's when Bayer started coating its tablets with a protective microcovering. Why did Bayer wait so long? "Tradition," said a Bayer spokeswoman. Tradition for Bayer meant being consistent. We trust Bayer Aspirin because it's familiar to us, and we choose it over chemically equivalent yet cheaper brands.

Politicians know the importance of being consistent with the expectations of voters. To remain consistent to their campaign promises not to increase taxes, presidents have gone to great lengths to avoid the T-word.

During the Reagan administration, an administration official referred to a four-cents-a-gallon increase in the federal gasoline tax as a "user fee" so as not to use the word *tax*. Trying to raise taxes without saying so, President Clinton announced that his proposed healthcare plan would be partially financed by a "wage-based premium"—in other words, a tax.

Heads Up

Asking the other person to retreat from her announced position is asking her to be inconsistent with herself. The New Revelation Tactic gives her a graceful way to retreat from her previously taken position.

Chapter Summary

Create interest in what you have to say, otherwise your argument won't be heard.

Call on comparison power because everything you say or suggest is relative.

It's not enough that the other guy feels you're credible. What you say has to sound credible. Things sound credible when they are precise. When you call on the power of "who else says so." The power of "if I can, you can too." And the power of appearing to be "in the know."

Lead with a story. Stories are easily understood, memorable, and compelling.

In the Consent Zone, the other person will find comfort and guidance in following your lead.

Everyone needs to be able to comfortably backpedal from their previously heels-dug-in position. The New Revelation Tactic does just that.

5

Create a Bulletproof Argument

Because winning requires "sounds right" reasoning

It's not enough that what you have to say feels right. It must also sound right. "Feeling right" is an emotional thing. "Sounding right" is a logic thing.

In this chapter you'll discover how to make things sound right with drop-'em-in-their-tracks content creation tactics.

"Logic is in the eye of the logician."

—Gloria Steinem

When the guys on the Wilson High quad weren't talking about girls, we were exploring the magic and mystery of logic. Can you find faulty logic in this classic story that has baffled me since 9th grade? Our math teacher, Mr. Huffman, had an explanation that still rings true: logic is both magical and mysterious.

· · · ·

It was a dark and stormy night. Seeking refuge from a worsening storm, three men—strangers to each other—race into a small hotel at the same time.

The clerk tells the three men that only one room is left. A $30 room. The men agree to share the room. Each man hands the clerk $10.

Minutes after going to the room, there's a knock on the door. It's the bellboy who says, "The desk clerk made a terrible mistake. The room is only $25." The bellboy then placed five $1 bills on a table.

Each man picked up a dollar. The remaining $2 was given to the bellboy as a tip.

The next day, one of the men told the story to his wife. "I originally paid $10, but I got back $1. So I paid $9 and contributed one-third of the $2 tip," he said.

"Wait a minute," she said. "Three times the $9 you each paid is $27. And the $2 tip the bellboy got makes it a total of $29. What happened to the other $1?"

Heads Up

Logic is both truth and fiction. Reality and illusion. Magic and mystery. What seems logical to me may not seem logical to you. Logic doesn't exist in the abstract but in the eye of the logician.

Craft a Core Argument
Because your argument must pass the Business Card Test

Have you ever walked out of a meeting without the faintest idea of what you were supposed to do? Or why you were there in the first place?

"Eric the Bore" was my co-chair for a charity fund-raiser. I spent a week with Eric one afternoon. At least it seemed like a week. Eric is a rambler who leaves nothing out and then repeats what he said. You know. A I-heard-you-twice-the-first-time kinda guy. Eric was quickly tuned out. It's more comfortable to jump to conclusions than suffer "death by a thousand words."

We need to "have our say" in order to vent our emotions, establish human contact, and feel in touch. We need to express ourselves to gain the approval of others, to display our intellect, and to give evidence of our skill and virtue. Great. So let me ask you this: just what do you expect to gain by using up someone else's valuable time to satisfy your personal needs?

Most of us say too much. We don't stick to the point. We tell others much more than they need or want to know. And we use 30 percent more words than are needed to drive our point home.

TV broadcasters know that attention spans are short. That we seldom have any desire to hear the whole story. Here's part of a television news-cast schedule that was broadcast to a region of three million viewers:

- Arrests made at crack house: 18 seconds.
- Suspect surrenders in shooting and robbery of tourist: 13 seconds.
- Teacher suspended for carrying concealed weapon: 59 seconds.
- Fire in Everglades almost out: 27 seconds.
- Lifeguards rescue 50 people from strong riptides: 17 seconds.
- Robbers nabbed outside grocery store: 23 seconds.
- Flooding in Illinois: 16 seconds.
- Attack of the tumbleweeds in New Mexico: 12 seconds.

Nelson Mandela made a speech on the day he was released from a South African prison after 27 years of confinement. The historic speech that marked the end to apartheid lasted less than five minutes.

People repeat themselves to emphasize their logic. But they end up over-expressing themselves. Impact increases with one or two repetitions of an idea. After that, your thoughts will be suffocated by too many words.

Are you getting ready to ramble? Tune into what you're saying. Here are a few red flags that you are about to over-express yourself: "To be quite honest with you...." "Basically...." "Essentially...." "Frankly...."

But what if you can't find just the right words? Silence is better than puffy fillers, go-nowhere words, *uhhs*, and *umms*. Recall the lesson of David and the Ancient Masters. A *still center* empowers you to have the sense of self-command to make your argument and then shut up. When do you stop? When you feel you've said *almost* enough.

BACK IN THE NEIGHBORHOOD...

"It's a trade-off: A multiplex means more traffic and more noise. On the other hand, you won't have to drive a few miles to see a movie on Saturday night."

A few cases in point:

The New Zealand captain of the *Exciter*—a super-fast Bay of Islands tour boat—had a warning for us passengers that was concise, clear, and most convincing: "Arms make a funny squishing sound when hung outside the boat while docking."

Some Americans who applauded air strikes in Afghanistan were opposed to putting U.S. ground troops in harm's way. A military spokesperson's compelling "boots on the ground" argument: "No one ever surrendered to an airplane."

The anti-rape campaign at Ohio State University produced brochures, pamphlets, and speeches. But 200 urinal screens were printed with what could best be described as a truly grabbing message: "You hold the power to stop rape in your hand."

• • • •

On a Greek island cruise, Gary, a ventriloquist, and his dummy, Homer, somehow said it all:

HOMER: I heard the President's speech last night. It lasted an
          hour and a half.
GARY: An hour and a half!!! What was his speech about?
HOMER: He didn't say.

Maybe Gary and Homer's routine was inspired by President John Adams's inaugural address. It had one sentence that was 727 words long! Confusing motion for progress, Fidel Castro began his speech to the United Nations by saying, "Although it has been said of us that we speak at great length, you may rest assured we shall endeavor to be brief." He then spoke for four hours and 29 minutes.

One day someone may try to present you with the Christopher Columbus Award. My advice: Turn away and run! The award is no honor. It's given to would-be persuaders who have no idea where they're going; upon arriving, don't know where they are; and when finishing up, haven't a clue where they've been.

The Business Card Test

To avoid being a Christopher Columbus Award recipient, the next time you seek to get others to think what you think, strive instead to pass the Business Card Test.

To start, write your *core argument* (why your neighbors should oppose the multiplex), on the back of a business card. If your core argument doesn't fit, then it's vague and uncertain. Work to clarify, sharpen, and simplify it.

Here's how to craft a core argument that passes the test...

You have facts and you have an analysis. Now ask yourself, *What do I conclude from all of this?* Once you reach your conclusion, you're still a ways from being done.

The next step is to ask yourself, *What do I conclude from that conclusion?* By repeating this process several more times, you will strip away all superfluous data, leaving only your core argument.

BACK IN THE NEIGHBORHOOD...

"*If a multiplex theater is built, our neighborhood will surely suffer.*"

If your core argument passes the Business Card Test, give yourself a pat on the back. It's never easy to turn your prize ox into a bouillon cube. Being able to accurately simplify your thoughts is an intellectual achievement.

My 5 Favorite Logic Tricks

Here are five of my favorite logic tricks for crafting a bulletproof core argument.

Logician Trick #1: *Craft a core argument by redefining the issue.*

If the subject is abortion, the big issue is whether the subject of the abortion is a "what" or a "who." If the subject is a "what" (something that isn't yet human), then a freedom of choice can be advocated. If you define the subject as a "who" (a human being), then abortion could be condemned as manslaughter.

Logician Trick #2: *Craft a core argument by redefining elements of the issue.*

Pro-choice advocates argue that you define a human as having characteristics A, B, C, and D. Because an embryo at the instant of conception has none of these characteristics, it's not yet human.

Pro-life activists argue that at the instant of conception, the embryo possesses all the genetic material necessary to be a human being.

Logician Trick #3: *Craft a core argument by redefining the scope of the issue.*

Pro-life advocates argue that if we kill defenseless embryos, how can *any* member of society expect to be treated with compassion and mercy?

Pro-choice advocates argue that if a woman is denied freedom of choice within her own body, how safe are *any* of our freedoms?

In both arguments, the issues are expanded. The scope of the argument is no longer simply the destiny of an embryo, but the larger issues of mercy, morality, compassion, and freedom.

Logician Trick #4: *Craft a core argument by showing an if/then correlation.*

Trace evidence of material used to make bombs was found in the wreckage of TWA Flight 800. The Paris-bound plane left New York and exploded off the coast of Long Island, killing all 230 people aboard. The conclusion reached by some experts: *if* there was bomb residue, *then* the plane was blown up. It was later determined that the telltale bomb residue was left by a U.S. military unit that had chartered the plane earlier.

Logician Trick #5: *Craft a core argument by expanding the realm of the possible.*

If something is possible without special effort, then it must be possible with effort: A small child easily learns Spanish when it is her native language. Certainly then, a non-Hispanic college student could easily learn Spanish. (*Author's note*: I am living proof of the fallacy of this logic. I faithfully attended class. Sought the help of Señora Shallenberger, a tutor, who gave soul and authenticity to my lessons by wearing a silver tiara and a black Spanish lace shawl. Despite all this, I died an excruciating death in Spanish 3.)

Tip

Getting others to buy into your logic begins with crafting a clear, concise core argument. To uncover your core argument, force yourself to repeatedly pare away the extraneous until all that's left passes the Business Card Test.

Support Your Core Argument with 3 Portable Points

Because too little is too little, and too much is too much

You've already met Greg, my stand-up comedy workshop instructor. Greg taught us that "the use of threes is a trick passed among comics as some mystical rule. A great joke is in the punch. In the unexpected. People think in patterns of three. Break the pattern's expectation and you'll get your punch—and hopefully some laughs."

A workshop example: "These dresses come in three sizes. Small, medium, and tent." (The humor doesn't come through when it's a four-word pattern: "Small, medium, large, and tent.")

Greg is right. There's a magic about threes. "Threes" are best remembered and carry max impact.

Advertisers know we're culturally attuned to messages that contain clusters of threes:

Live, love, eat.

—Wolfgang Puck Cafes

No battery. Quartz accuracy. Revolutionary.

—Seiko Kinetic Watches

Trustworthy. Reliable. Friendly.
—Ricoh Business Machines

Funk, Fashion & Fettuccine.
—Hollywood's Famed Sunset Strip

Italian. Sensual. Warm.
—Disaronno Amaretto

Invisible. Inaudible. Incredible.
—Comanche Stealth Helicopters

Snap, Crackle, Pop.
—Rice Krispies

Real Food. Real Life. Real Results.
—Weight Watchers

Write down the three main points that support your core argument—reasons *why* the other person should buy into your core argument. To maximize impact, ask yourself: *What do I know? What do they know? What do they need to know?* The best points are what I call *portable points*—three points out of all the possibilities that you would like the other person to "take home."

BACK IN THE NEIGHBORHOOD...

"There are three reasons why we must say No to a multiplex.

1. Traffic will make our street more congested. more dangerous, and more noisy.
2. Property values will decrease as the character of the neighborhood becomes more commercial.
3. Fast-food franchises and other high-traffic businesses will find it desirable to open near the multiplex. making things even worse."

A Pig Farmer's Heads Up

But what if you have more than three main points? It's best not to strut all your stuff at one time. A case in point:

> A farmer owned a pig that once saved a child from being run over by a speeding car. A pig known to have ushered a family from their burning cottage. The farmer was asked, "You have an amazing pig, but why does he have a peg leg?"
>
> "When you have a pig this great, you don't eat him all at once!" he answered.

In school, we learned that A's went to those students whose reports had the most points. A+'s went to those who could back up those points with zillions of footnotes. Your English teacher *had* to read your report. That's what she was paid to do. The people you want to influence *don't have to* tune into your argument. And if it isn't compelling, they won't.

With an argument that has more than three points, the important and the unimportant soon meld into a brain-deadening blur. With less than three points, your logic may appear flimsy and lacking. But logic with three supporting points discourages rebuttal and takes on powerful clarity.

How to Make Complex Points Simple

There'll be times when your core argument will be supported by *complex points*. Here's how the pros present complex points:

Break up the complex point. This will yield a pile of parts. These parts may be called steps, phases, or sections. Immediately after presenting an individual part, explain why it's important.

The result is a powerful layered effect: presentation of a part...explanation of why that part is important...presentation of another part...explanation of how that part interfaces with the previous part and why it, too, is important...and so on.

Play Your Points by the Numbers

You've discovered that having three portable points in support of your core argument is a highly effective tool. To power up your portable points, play them out by the numbers.

You'll see what I mean when you compare these two plays:

PLAY 1: There are important reasons for us to oppose the
multiplex....

PLAY 2: There are three important reasons for us to oppose the
multiplex....

Play 1 is humdrum and flat. Play 2 is seductive—a listener will want to listen, to focus, to start writing what you're about to say. A reader will quicken his or her reading pace to discover what the pages ahead have in store.

There's only one difference between the two plays: the number *3*. The actual number isn't important. I was induced to read the following articles because of their intriguing numbered themes: "5 Ways to Quickly Lose Weight," "Professional Photographers Share Their 10 Best Tips," "6 Deadly Phrases That Will Kill Any Deal." Could you have flipped past any of these articles without giving them a chance to strut their stuff?

Tip

Using numbers to identify your portable points ("One, traffic will...." "Two, property values will....") gives you a firm grasp over the presentation of your ideas and makes it easier for a listener or reader to track your thinking.

Getting others to buy into your logic isn't about sandbagging them with every point you can think of. It's about creating a crystal-clear *core argument* supported by three numbered *portable points*.

Logic's 3 Biggest Traps

Because you want your logic to be bulletproof

Trap #1: *Illustrations are not proof*. ("Let me tell you what happened last Saturday night at the Riverdale multiplex....")

An example can be found to support any point you make. Refuting examples can be found just as readily. It's risky to dwell on any *one* example. When you don't have conclusive proof, use an *assortment* of short, simple examples to back up your conclusion.

Trap #2: *Common knowledge is not evidentiary.* ("Everyone knows what happens when multiplexes open in quiet neighborhoods....")

All it takes to refute the statement "everyone knows..." is to name one person who doesn't know.

Trap #3: *The general is not powerful.*

It's the specific that empowers others to envision what you envision. To be concerned about what concerns you. *"Traffic problems come with multiplexes"* is a conclusion. It doesn't hammer home your point the same way as a specific statement: *"Studies reveal that traffic in and around a six-screen theater can increase 20-fold on a weekend."*

Chapter Summary

Logic is both magical and mysterious. Drop-'em-in-their-tracks logic begins with a core argument supported with three portable numbered points.

6

Know What to Say, When to Say It, and What Not to Say

Because every argument has slippery slopes

In this chapter you'll discover eight business-as-usual argument moves. But how they play out may not be to your liking.

The Green Machine was a team of 7-year-old AYSO soccer players. My daughter Melissa was a Green Machine player. The Titans were their rivals.

Todd was a Titan. During one very close game, Todd's father ran up and down the sidelines screaming, "Todd, you're not hustling!" "Run! Run!! Run!!!" "Todd, keep your eye on the ball!" I felt embarrassed for Todd. But what should or could I do?

Finally, my neighbor John cupped his hands and shouted across the playing field, "If you want Todd to be a champion, you'll have to yell a lot louder than that!"

Meet Libby and Sam

Because they argue with Sue about schoolwork

Our high schooler, Sue, is bright and capable. That's the good news. The bad news is that just about everything takes a priority over homework.

We've tried the usual approaches: "Please, I can't take it anymore. You've got to do your homework" and "What am I going to do with you?" What arguments can we possibly make to convince Sue to get serious about school?

From bookstore signings and radio show call-ins, it was clear what moms and dads in cities and towns big and small were thinking. When presented with similar scenarios, here are the supposedly "cool moves" and "hot tips" suggested by call-in audiences:

1. *Liking*: Be incredibly nice to Sue so she will feel obligated to reciprocate by studying more.

2. *Specific payoff to be earned*: "Sue, if you study more, I'll increase your allowance by half."

3. *Punishment to be imposed*: "Sue, if you don't study more, I'll cut your allowance in half."

4. *Personal betterment*: "Sue, if you study more, it will be your gain because you'll have bettered yourself."

5. *Loss of betterment*: "Sue, not studying is your loss because you're not living up to your potential."

6. *Specific payoff in advance of compliance*: "Sue, I'm raising your allowance by half, but I expect you to study much more."

7. *Specific punishment in advance of compliance*: "Sue, I'm cutting your allowance in half until you start studying more."

8. *Personal satisfaction*: "Sue, by studying harder you'll feel better about yourself knowing you have given school your all."

9. *Loss of satisfaction*: "Sue, if you don't study you'll go through life blaming yourself for not having given the best you have to give."

10. *Appeal to morality*: "Sue, it's morally wrong not to study so you can be all you can possibly be."

11. *Appeal to popular opinion*: "Sue, your family and friends will be so proud of you if you get good grades."

12. *Fear of rejection*: "Sue, the family will be so disappointed if you don't get good grades."

13. *Personal request*: "Sue, I want you to get into a good college. As a favor to me, I want you to study harder."

14. *Sense of indebtedness*: "Sue, I am sacrificing so you don't need to work after school. You owe it to me to study harder and get good grades."

15. *Logic*: "Sue, college graduates earn much more than nongraduates. With that extra income you'll be able to have a much nicer home, car, and clothes."

16. *Appeal to self-esteem*: "Sue, a smart and mature person would want to study to make the most of herself."

17. *Threat to self-esteem*: "Sue, it would be irresponsible and immature of you not to take full advantage of a wonderful education."

Some of these suggestions are bribes. Some are warm and fuzzy pitches. Others are bullying, whining, wheedling, plodding, prodding, threatening, intimidating, disparaging, minimizing, or strong-arming.

Which of these 17 argument plays would you choose? Which of these plays have you used in arguments? Which ones worked well for you? Which ones did not?

Quick Quiz

How would you argue if Sue were your daughter?

Was your answer...

A *logic play*? You can tell Sue the reasons she should study. But people reacting emotionally don't always respond to logic. Logic is a response to Sue's reasons *given* rather than Sue's reasons *not disclosed*.

A *domination play*? ("You cannot...." "I insist that you...." "You are required to...." "My policy is....") A domination play is an invitation to a power struggle. A "because I'm the mommy, that's why" argument is only effective when the parties both recognize and accept the power relationship.

"Sue, you'll loose your driving privileges unless you study four hours a day" may get immediate action, but it's counterproductive in the long run. There's a difference between winning Sue's *compliance* and winning her *commitment*. Sue's fear of losing car privileges will lead to resentment. It won't lead to a true change.

A *negotiation play*? To negotiate is to compromise. By their very nature, negotiations may lead to a result where neither Mom and Dad nor Sue is completely satisfied. Besides, negotiating an agreement that Sue will study two hours each evening may not be enough to get the job done.

An *incentive play*? Giving Sue an incentive to study "tonight" or "to study all week" won't produce long-term results. You may be able to implement a long-term incentive program, but will it result in Sue developing good study habits? If there is going to be an incentive, the choice of the incentive has to be yours, not Sue's. ("Sue, don't get the impression I owe you something for doing your homework. Whether or not I offer you a reward is my choice, not yours.")

Heads Up

Salespeople are coached to introduce incentives by asking questions rather than touting the benefits their product or service has to offer. ("What if you could cut your telephone long-distance rates by 35 percent?")

A *threatening play*? ("You really don't want me to...." "You're forcing me to...." "You'll be sorry if you....") I was in a room where lawyers were finger-pointing and threatening each other with all sorts of retaliation. Finally, one lawyer took a deep breath, and after a few moments of silence said, "Now that we've gone through all of the 'don't-mess-with-me-I-know-karate stuff,' let's get down to business."

There are too many "never evers" in life to begin with: *never ever* stand until the captain turns off the seat belt sign...*never ever* flirt in the workplace...*never ever* kiss dogs on the lips...*never ever* buy dented canned goods...*never ever* use a radar detector (the cops get seriously annoyed when they pull you over and see one)...*never ever* hog the remote...and so on. Nonetheless, I have to add a few more to the list:

Never ever make a threat without first casting it as a *soft-touch warning*. ("Sue, if you don't study, I'll have no choice but to consider cutting your allowance.")

Never ever make a threat you don't want to carry out. Don't threaten to kick Sue out of the house if that is the last thing you would ever want to do.

Never ever use a big threat in furtherance of a small gain. Telling Sue that if her grades don't improve she "will never go out on Saturday night again" won't sound credible under any circumstances. Your threat has to be proportional to its purpose and objective.

A *catastrophe-avoidance play*? I was 30 years old when my first child, Steve, was born. No sooner had the cigars been passed out than I was confronted by an endless stream of life insurance salespeople. All of them had the same pitch: If I died, Steve might not be able to go to college. My family could be forced to move to a place where danger lurked in every corner. And my wife, Bev, would be forced to work long hours just to make ends meet.

I didn't buy into their arguments and held off buying life insurance until I was in my late 30s. Waiting may or may not have been the wise thing to do. But then, at the time my first child was born, I couldn't envision anything other than immortality. The probability of dropping dead in my tracks was beyond my contemplation.

In my freshman philosophy class, we dealt with this thorny question: Suppose state highway patrol officers no longer issued speeding tickets. Instead, a single officer would roam the highways with strict orders to summarily execute anyone caught speeding. Would our highways be safer because of the possibility of on-the-spot execution?

It is not enough to present a risk. The other person must feel that the risk is real. The class agreed that the chance of being caught was so remote that the risk of execution was almost nonexistent. There is a difference between a possibility and a probability.

You can tell Sue that if she doesn't study she'll never be all she can be. But Sue won't be motivated unless she buys into the probability of that really happening.

A *strong-arm play*? Getting Sue to hit the books is not about strong-arming her. If Sue is verbally strong-armed, she'll feel bitter. Resentful. She'll look for get-even opportunities.

An *accommodation play*? Most of us avoid confrontations because they result in anger, defensiveness, or rejection. An accommodation play means giving into Sue's refusal to study. You're responding to Sue's emotions, but you're not managing them.

Chapter Summary

Groping along in dense coastal fog is part of being a Maine lobsterman.

"How do you know where the rocks are?" newsman Walter Cronkite asked a lobsterman.

"Don't," he replied. "I know where they ain't."

7

Assemble an Arsenal of Magic Words and Phrases

Because the way to win is to grab, hold, and convince

Call upon words and phrases to zoom your argument from flabby and ho-hum dull to captivating and compelling.

In this chapter you'll discover how the pros present things not as they are, but as they want them to be perceived.

It's Power-Upper Time
Because you want to "caffeinate" your argument

You'll need a basic black dress that will always get you out of a what-to-wear jam. Jazz it up with a glittery necklace, glitzy shoes, and a gold belt, and you're off and ready for the party.

—A Fashion Editor's Advice for Young Women Heading Off for Their First Year of College

How can you power up a phrase, a sentence, or a paragraph to make it so seductive and so powerful that it reaches, grabs, holds, and convinces?

How can you power up words to slam-dunk a point?

How can you power up your portable points to make them more intriguing, memorable, and easily understood?

It's easy. Abandon the anemic, the rote, the stilted, and the stuffy. *Power-uppers* "jazz up" your basic plain-wrap argument.

Power-Upper #1: *Craft analogies.*

> *The companies that succeed will be the ones that*
> *make their ideas real...that employ great metaphors*
> *and analogies to define their businesses and tell*
> *their stories.*

—Scott McNealy, Cofounder of Sun Microsystems

Ideas become explosive when you call upon the awesome power of analogies.

Microsoft monopolized the Internet-browser market by bundling its browser with its Windows operating system—a market in which it already had a monopoly. With that allegation, the Department of Justice demanded that Microsoft bundle two browsers, its own and Netscape's, or none at all. Bill Gates's powerful analogy compared the demand to "requiring Coke to ship two cans of Pepsi with every six-pack."

It's not a beautiful city and the traffic is terrible. The air is thick with humidity and mosquitoes. But then Houston is a city built on a swamp. A local marketing firm launched an online campaign seeking ways to promote Houston without resorting to catchphrases that really didn't say much. A sampling of some that were used and then soon abandoned: "Houston Proud." "Houston's Hot." "Space City. A Space of Infinite Possibilities."

A local seemed to have said it all with an analogy that captured national attention: "If Houston were a dog, she'd be a mutt with three legs, one bad eye, fleas the size of CornNuts, and buckteeth. Despite all that, she'd be the best dog you'd ever know."

Many feel that the U.S. military response to the World Trade Center attack should have been limited to the capture of Osama bin Laden and his henchmen. A White House official used a stand-up-and-take-notice analogy to argue why that wasn't a real alternative to war: "You don't get rid of a mosquito problem by swatting mosquitoes. You get rid of it by draining the swamp."

"Hot analogies" are used to rouse and stir emotions. Those who favored the United States going to war in Iraq likened Saddam Hussein to Adolph Hitler. Those opposed warned that we were getting into "another Vietnam."

Power-Upper #2: *Impact with intensifiers.*

Intensifiers are descriptive words that create visual images. Attention-garnering snapshots that pique interest, making listeners and readers want to learn more.

O.J. Simpson's defense witnesses used a memorable phrase that damaged the prosecution. The witness, a DNA expert, called the Los Angeles Police Department's lab a "cesspool of contamination." Anyone who has ever been near a cesspool readily recalls the sensory, nose-pinching experience.

Intensifiers cause the other person to recall an experience of sight, sound, smell, taste, touch, pain, or pleasure. The television show *Law & Order* pitches that its plotlines have been "ripped from the headlines."

Convincing guys they need cleanser and moisturizer as much as women is a challenge. A men's skincare company met the challenge by coaching department store salespeople: "Men relate to cars and sports, so use words like *tackle acne*." The line's products include "Fix" (to clear up acne) and "Restore" (an under-eye puffiness reducer).

Power-Upper #3: *Tantalize with the unexpected.*

Retire the lame and overworked. Trash the trite. Make what's old seem fresh.

Today you can buy "genuine" draft beer ("Miller Genuine Draft"), cars ("Genuine Chevrolet"), and underwear ("Genuine Jockey"). Even rhythm and blues artist Elgin Lumpkin has—if you'll excuse the pun—gotten into the act. To show that he's the real thing, Elgin has trademarked a new name: "Ginuwine."

Where do you find words that snap and sparkle? Take a look at billboard and magazine ads. Which words grab you? Which words make you want to learn more? Which words make you smile?

Power-Upper #4: *Replace dull numbers with grabbers.*

Logic can be dull. Look how numbing, dry statistics can become grabbers—attention-getters that are understood, dramatic, and remembered.

> *Enough Cracker Jack has been sold to stretch end-to-end more than 63 times around the world.*
>
> —Cracker Jack Package

*Tootsie Roll makes enough candy each year to stretch
from the Earth to the Moon and back.*

—Associated Press

*There are 25 million acres of lawn in the U.S.—about
the size of Pennsylvania.*

—*Forbes*

Mercedes-Benz introduced its new "super-luxury" Maybach auto-mobile. *Car and Driver* dramatized its sky-high sticker price: "You can actually get 22 Toyota Corollas for the price of our test car."

Here's how *Newsweek* brought home what Bill Gates's wealth meant in everyday terms: Gates could buy each household in the United States a new 27-inch color television or put a new Honda Accord LX in the garage of each Washington State household.

The *Wall Street Journal* calculated that if Gates paid the same percentage of his net worth for a movie ticket that the average Joe pays, the ticket would cost him $19 million.

The American Federation of Labor–Congress of Industrial Organizations dramatically demonstrated the difference in compensation between CEOs and ordinary working folks: If you're a hot-dog vendor at Disneyland making minimum wage, you'd have to work 17,852 years to equal Disney's Chief Executive Officer Michael Eisner's then compensation package. An employee of Coca-Cola who earns $35,000 a year would have to work 207 years to earn as much as Roberto Goizueta, its late CEO.

Power-Upper #5: *Call upon persuasion-speak words.*

Here's how to take the "rocky" out of rocky road...

The snack package served to me on a Southwest Airlines flight contained crackers, cheese, summer sausage, and a Kellogg's Nutri-Grain bar. The package said it was distributed by "Oakfield Farms." *Oakfield* and *Farms*—words that create an image of grassy hills, white fences, and majestic oaks. Oakfield Farms never had acreage, but it does have an office in Los Angeles. My snack package reminded me of the home builder who chopped down each and every one of the trees on his 10-acre tract and then named his development "Shady Oaks."

A new law client explained that she scouts the fashion capitals of Europe in search of women's handbags, which—with the exception of the designers' names and logos—she faithfully reproduces in China for mass distribution. My mistake was asking a question that began, "When you *copy* these originals...." She cut me off in mid-sentence with a smile and a wink: "I don't think of myself as 'copying' or 'knocking off' someone else's designs. I merely *reinterpret* what they have done."

As an ensign on the *USS Helena*, I could either *dine* in the officers' wardroom or *eat* in the enlisted personnel's mess hall. I almost always headed to the wardroom. Sunday morning breakfast was the exception. The wardroom served the tired, trite, and true: bacon and eggs, pancakes and eggs, grits and eggs. But the mess hall served up what was a Sunday morning tradition: fried chicken and eggs. Breakfast a mega-leap beyond the wardroom's Denny's-type fare.

I looked forward to my Sunday morning fried chicken and eggs. Until it happened. The big turnoff. One Sunday, I heard a food server yelling to a cook, "We need more mother and daughter." To this day, I still don't have an appetite for the combination dish of fried chicken and eggs.

Canned soup labeled "homestyle" is cooked up in an inner-city plant where workers wearing scrubs, caps, and gloves pour artificial flavoring and chemical additives into monster mixing vats. We're asked to accept the end product as "old-fashioned goodness." Of course, there's always the dehydrated, just-add-boiling-water "gourmet dining in a cup" alternative.

A deli client of mine serves zillions of bowls of "homemade" chicken noodle soup. One day, Lenny needed to talk to me privately about a pressing legal problem. We went into the deli's kitchen where yellow food coloring was being poured into a steaming pot of chicken soup. "Homemade"? Mom never had to yellow-up her chicken soup.

Store windows were shattered. Kids and adults were grabbing stereos, athletic shoes, and anything else they could carry, cart, or haul. There was rioting in a Los Angeles neighborhood, and people who would normally never dream of stealing were stealing like crazy.

One teenager cradling a cardboard box in his arms was ambushed by an in-your-face reporter: "What are you stealing?"

The thief snapped, "I'm not stealing!! I'm looting."

Steal. Loot. Just words?

Steal is a harsh-sounding word. From its tone, you know someone is up to no good. But *loot* has a softer sound. Its tone is gentle. Melodic. Suggestive of conduct more mischievous than criminal. Maybe that's why "lying" is bad but "fudging" about the truth is, well, less bad.

Companies "out-placing" personnel has looped into trendy downsizing lingo to side-step telling employees "You're fired!" Being plain kissed-off has been called "release of resources" (Bank of America)..."rightsizing"

(Harris Bank of Chicago)..."repositioning" (Stanford University)..."reducing duplication" (Tandem Computers).

Dumps on the outskirts of cities are now called "landfills." The word *landfill* creates an image of *filling* the land rather than dumping things onto it.

It's tough to get federal appropriation money to protect yucky "swamps." So how do you go about saving swamps? By calling them "wetlands."

Pornography is soft-pedaled as "adult entertainment." Strippers as "exotic dancers."

Wanting to appeal to conservative investors, casino operators have transformed Las Vegas from a town that "gambles" to one that "games."

We associate "used cars" with problems. "Transportation counselors" (formerly car salesmen) no longer sell used cars. Instead, they sell "previously owned cars." It's the perceived difference between a beat-up heap and a pampered chariot.

"Used" can also be turned into chichi. Goodwill "the thrift shop" is trying to convince us that it's now Goodwill "the fashion store." Goodwill stores are becoming a destination of choice rather than one of need by playing down "cheap" and playing up "vintage"—by advertising worn jeans as "broken-in jeans," shrunken T-shirts as "retro shirts," beat-up leather jackets as "distressed leather jackets."

Comedian Dennis Miller argues that opponents of capital punishment would be less resistant if we relabeled the death penalty a "life relinquishment program."

Bankers don't tell their shareholders they made "bad loans." They just have "nonperforming assets."

At the Hertz counter, a Ford Taurus is called a "full-size" car. A full-size car, the Ford Crown Victoria, is called "premium."

A shop down the street advertises a box spring and mattress set as a "sleep system."

My friend Jim is overweight. "Obese," if you want to be clinical. "Fat," if you call 'em as you see 'em. But Jim calls himself neither. Instead he's a "champion in the war against anorexia." Too stubborn to go on a diet, Jim's doctor has put him on a "food program."

At a seminar, salespeople were taught that "customers are terrified of sales jargon...so say 'visit' instead of 'appointment.' 'Paperwork' instead of 'contract.' And 'autograph' instead of 'signature.'"

Hasbro insisted that its G.I. Joe is not a doll. At the time, the U.S. tariff code put higher duties on dolls than other toys. Disagreeing, a Customs Court judge ruled that, for customs purposes, Joe was indeed a doll. But Hasbro knows that a boy usually wouldn't play with a doll. Once G.I. Joe cleared customs, he became an "action figure."

When the Miami Heat tied its own NBA record for scoring the fewest points in a game, coach Pat Riley didn't say the Heat's performance was awful. Or terrible. Or dreadful. Taking the rocky out of rocky road, Riley told the press that the Heat had suffered "skill erosion."

Having a cool name for a project is "part of getting people excited enough to work 70 hours a week," confides a former Apple engineer. Chip-maker Advanced Micro Devices (AMD) runs second to its competitor, Intel. The cool project name for its first 64-bit chip for mid-size computers was SledgeHammer. A name that suggested AMD's new product was going to pound Intel. When SledgeHammer was ready to ship, it was renamed Opteron.

The cool name for a Microsoft set of Internet functions was HailStorm. Because Microsoft's aggressive business practices were under fire, the product suite was renamed .Net My Services.

Choosing the right words is a powerful logic tool. But get too carried away and you'll lose credibility. When a cruise missile crashed in 1986, the U.S. Air Force announced that it had "impacted with the ground prematurely."

Argument pros are wordsmiths. Don't call it as you see it. Call it as you want the other guy to see it. The words and names you choose will impact how the other person feels about swamps, summer sausage, and the project he or she is spending endless hours working on.

Power-Upper #6: *Craft persuasion-speak labels.*

> *He was a terrorist, not a patriot, they concluded—*
> *and he deserved to die.*
>
> —*Newsweek* on the Trial of Oklahoma City
> Bomber Timothy J. McVeigh

Civilians are often killed by bombs. Sometimes the people doing the bombing are U.S. airmen flying combat missions. Other times they're militants detonating explosives on trains, in office buildings, or on city streets.

Whether it's the airman or whether it's Timothy McVeigh, someone who intentionally sets off a bomb is a "bomber." That's a neutral and undeniable statement of fact. That bomber is also something more: a "guerilla," a "soldier," a "terrorist," a "patriot."

That "something more" is in the eyes of the beholder. The bomber, labeled a "freedom fighter" by some, will be labeled a "murderer" by others.

Until someone comes along with a label, the bomber is still just a bomber. If I tell you the bomber is a patriot and you believe me, you will think and react differently than if I tell you he is a terrorist. But those who dispatched the terrorist on his mission will see him as a hero.

The label "terrorist" was never used in Reuters news stories about those responsible for the 9-11 tragedy. Except when it quoted others who were using the "T" label, the acclaimed news service opted instead for benign phrases such as "hard-line Afghan Islamists" and "hard-line Taliban." The reason? "Terrorist" is an emotionally loaded label. A judgmental label. Reuters provides stories to newspapers and media subscribers worldwide, and many throughout Islam saw the World Trade Center perpetrators as heroes or warriors rather than terrorists.

What was your attitude about Vietnam war protests? Did you unthinkingly buy into what others told you—that the protesters were nothing more than "anti-American agitators"? When Washington hesitated over Kosovo or Bosnia, did you say we were refusing to lead? When our bombers flew, did you say they were the leading edge of American imperialism? Did you readily accept President Reagan's label that Russia was the "Evil Empire" or President George W. Bush's label that Iraq, Iran, and North Korea are the "Axis of Evil"?

Be a label-smith. Craft labels that will prompt others to think what you think and see what you see.

Chapter Summary

Call upon words, phrases, and labels that propel your argument downfield. The six *Power-Uppers* grab attention. Highlight key concepts. Bring clarity to your argument. Zoom your points home, making them memorable and easily shared.

CHAPTER

8

Craft Surgical Strike Questions

Because the other person's answers will be your desired outcome

In this chapter you'll discover a true-to-life dialogue showing how questions asked, rather than statements made, win arguments. It's what argument pros call *slow squeezing*.

You won't help shoots grow by pulling them higher.

—Chinese Proverb

This chapter isn't about China. It's about what happened to us in the former Yugoslavia. Bev and I arrived in Zagreb, in the former Yugoslavia, on a Saturday night in November. In our room at the InterContinental Hotel was a brochure extolling the beauty of Plitvice Lakes—16 small lakes connected by waterfalls, in a beautiful mountain setting.

A Sunday visit to Plitvice Lakes sounded wonderful. According to the concierge, Plitvice Lakes tour buses did not operate off-season, but public buses ran in each direction on the hour. The journey, which would take two and a half hours, cost $2.50—a true bargain. We were concerned about the weather, but the concierge assured us the tram that circled the lakes every 45 minutes was enclosed, and that a "visit to the lakes was an absolute must."

We arrived at the lakes at 1 p.m., only to discover that every restaurant and shop was locked until summer. The tram ran only every three hours in the off-season, and the next tram was two hours later. Suddenly it began raining. I'm not talking drizzle, I'm talking buckets. With no place to go, we raced back to the main highway to catch the 2 p.m. return bus.

It gets worse.

There was no 2 p.m. bus. The 3 p.m. bus and the 4 p.m. bus passed us by. They were too filled with villagers returning to their jobs in Zagreb after a weekend at home.

By 4:30, we were very concerned, anxious, and wet. There were no taxis, there were no buses, there were no restaurants. There was coldness, there was rain, there was darkness.

Sloshing down the highway, we came across a local man who offered to drive us back to the hotel for $85. I was too wet and cold to think about negotiating, and I gladly accepted without a whimper.

Before going up to my hotel room, I stopped at the assistant manager's desk, feeling some sense of drama as I stood before him soaking wet. Certainly he would be sympathetic to the plight of a shivering guest.

I was wrong. He was unprepared to reimburse me the $85 or offer even a hot bowl of soup. He did agree to explain the situation to Mr. Bratas, the manager, when he arrived in the morning.

Here's the next morning's dialogue between Mr. Bratas and me:

MANAGER: I have received a memo from the assistant manager explaining in detail what happened. We regret the inconvenience. The hotel, however, does not take any responsibility for what happened.

BOB: Mr. Bratas, you may be right in what you are saying.

Acknowledging that Bratas *may be right* was both a defusing tactic and a modulating device, setting a tone for calm, nonpositional dialogue. It was also demonstrative of my having an open mind. Having a *still center* was critical. Criticizing or yelling would only have caused Bratas to become more defensive.

Addressing Bratas by name, I was both *personalizing* the link-up and reminding Bratas that he was an *active participant* in the problem-resolution process. I didn't want him to sit in silent judgment while I spun my tale of woe.

BOB: Perhaps I am totally wrong in asking the InterContinental to reimburse me. The hotel brochure in my room encourages visits to Plitvice Lakes. Your concierge told us that it would be a wonderful, relaxing way to spend our Sunday. Am I wrong in believing that the hotel was recommending a visit to the lakes?

Bratas had been invited to be both candid and objective with me. I needed Bratas to become involved, to evaluate the situation *with* me as part of a collaborative, nonadversarial effort. To accomplish an affecting-and-being-affected connection, I sincerely solicited Bratas's criticism of both my facts and my analysis of those facts. A position-oriented approach was painstakingly avoided.

Wanting Bratas to reciprocate, I was allowing my conclusions to be tested by his sense of what is fair and reasonable.

BOB: I appreciate the time that was taken by your staff in explaining how to take the bus to the lakes and back. Their interest and desire to be helpful is not in question.

Staff personalities had been separated from the argument. By telling Bratas that his staff tried to be cooperative and helpful, I was setting a hotel pattern of conduct and hospitality that I expected him to abide by. If brought into our discussions, the concierge would not think my quarrel was with him personally.

BOB: Hopefully you and the InterContinental will want to be fair with me. I don't want to appear greedy, and I know you too want to resolve this situation in a manner that is both sensible and fair.

Fairness, not money, was my primary stated concern. Bratas would fault such an approach. Not wanting to sound self-righteous, I didn't say, "Sure, the money is important, but even more important to me is whether I am being fairly treated."

BOB: Perhaps I should really be discussing my feelings with the InterContinental's management in the United States. To whom do you recommend that I write? Do you think it would help if my travel agent also wrote?

This *veiled ultimatum* reminded Bratas that I was serious about this situation and that the problem would not end with our discussion. I was not "reporting" him to management, but I did want to discuss my *feelings* with management. Bratas was on notice that he would have to continue to deal with the problem.

BOB: Mr. Bratas, I understand that your position is that you have no obligation to reimburse me the $85 I spent.

By acknowledging that I fully comprehend Bratas's position, I was *confirming* that I understood what he had said without *agreeing* with what he had said. By not having to reassert his position of nonresponsibility, he would perhaps be less defensive.

The words *you* and *your* rather than *hotel* were being used. Even though personalities were purposely being kept out of the picture, it was still very much a person-to-person dilemma.

BOB: I'm curious. What is the reason you do not want to reimburse me?

My question generously presupposed that Bratas has a rationale for his stated position. This may or may not be true, but the approach would compel him to show his cards and produce the logic behind his stated position.

My *core argument* was that I was misled and, therefore, the hotel needed to reimburse me. My *three portable points* were cast as *surgical strike questions* that would cause Bratas to respond to my logic.

BOB: Let me ask a few questions to make absolutely sure I understand the facts:
- Is the brochure in every room because the hotel recommends visits to Plitvice Lakes?
- Is it the duty of your concierge to assist guests with local touring?
- Should the concierge have dissuaded rather than encouraged us from going to the lakes?

These pointed questions were designed to elicit answers that I knew already. The questions forced Bratas to rethink the fairness and logic behind his stated position. If Bratas was to change his mind, it would be because of *questions asked* rather than *statements* made.

BOB: I think I understand what you're saying. The hotel has no responsibility to me because it has no control over whether buses are filled or Plitvice Lakes facilities are closed. If my understanding is wrong, please tell me.

Again, I had confirmed in positive, unsarcastic terms that I understood what Bratas told me. He had now been invited to tell me whether my perceptions were wrong—a reminder that I wanted our communications to be open and clear. More importantly, the logic and rationale behind Bratas's position had been identified and contained. This "logic" could now be openly dealt with by both of us.

Questions rather than *statements* were posed to Bratas, causing him to respond with answers rather than defensive retorts. Questions also caused Bratas to remain an involved participant in my argument's *persuasive progression*.

BOB: I know you're trying to be fair with me.

Reminding Bratas that fairness is the standard of a mutually agreeable solution, I wanted him to continue to be worthy of my appreciation of what he, as a person, was trying to accomplish.

Bob: The suggestion to visit the lakes was the hotel's suggestion, which was reinforced by your concierge. The concierge also knew it was off-season, so the regular tour buses would not be operating again until summer.

Do you think it's reasonable for me to expect that he would have known Plitvice Lakes had become a desolate, off-season area?

You're right that a concierge has the job to assist hotel guests with their travel plans. I agree with you that he probably didn't know returning buses on Sundays would be too full to stop at the lakes for passengers. *What*, however, is the reason for the concierge not knowing the status of a hotel-recommended attraction?

I had to deal with a behavioral truth: it's more important for people to be right rather than reasonable. I have reaffirmed that what Bratas told me earlier was "right." Bratas wasn't being cross-examined in front of a judge or jury. He alone would decide whether I would be a winner. If Bratas was going to change his mind, it would be for his own reasons, not mine. My job was to cause him to generate his own reasons for wanting to change.

Using the word *what* rather than *why* kept an important question from having an accusatory quality.

> Bob: One fair method of resolving this situation would be for the hotel to reimburse us the $85 we spent, minus the cost of two return bus trips and the cost of taxi fare from the bus station back to the hotel. Do you think that makes sense?

A possibility had been presented for Bratas's evaluation. The proposed situation was not tendered as being mine or his. Instead, it *evolved* from our general dialogue without any claim of authorship. If it was rejected, it was not *my* proposal being refused, which would make it easier for me to try other possibilities.

The proposal was made only *after* the reasoning supporting the proposal had been communicated.

> Bob: If we are able to agree, then you can adjust my hotel bill. If we are unable to reach a satisfactory resolution to this situation, then I would like to discuss the matter further with whomever you believe to be the appropriate person in the United States.

I had reiterated that a No would not be conclusive. Although I didn't want to sound threatening, I did want Bratas to know where he stood with me. A harsh threat or clear warning, however, would only have destroyed the tone of objectivity I had created.

Wanting to make a positive answer as easy as possible for Bratas, I had suggested crediting my bill rather than writing a check or reimbursing me in cash. *Adjust* is a word associated with fairness and reason.

After Bratas consented to adjust the bill, I suggested it would be a nice goodwill gesture if my wife and I dined at the hotel that evening. Bratas agreed that it would, and it is with fondness that I still remember the cherry strudel.

Chapter Summary

Surgical strike questions cause the other guy to see for himself why it makes sense to see or do something your way.

9

Cinch Consent

Because it's now time to slam-dunk your win

People act and react in highly predictable ways as they quest to satisfy their emotional needs.

In this chapter you'll discover how to awaken, trigger, and stimulate conscious and subconscious emotional needs— needs that can be satisfied by your argument's desired outcome. You will also learn how to cinch consent with your "call for action."

A Lesson from an Airport Men's Room

Because you want to create and direct energy

Call them tendencies. Predispositions. Impulses. Our preprogrammed subconscious responses to what goes on around us.

Some tendencies come naturally...

Negri's Occidental Hotel is located in Sonoma County, California. A bold sign above the urinals in its men's room reads "STAND CLOSE."

It's not nice to look. But if it's for the sake of science, it's not "looking" or "peeking." It's "observing." And nobody I observed was obeying Negri's instruction.

The tiles under the urinals at the JFK Airport Arrivals Building have a "familiar lemony tinge; rubber-soled shoes will stick to it," reported the *Wall Street Journal.* But at Amsterdam's Schiphol Airport, the tiles under the urinals would pass an army sergeant's eagle-eyed inspection. The difference isn't in the mopping. The difference is urinal flies. At Schiphol, each urinal has a fly in it—actually, the black outline of a fly, etched into the porcelain. The fly "improves the aim. If a man sees a fly, he aims at it," a Schiphol executive explained. The fly etchings "reduce spillage by 80 percent." Schiphol's etched fly is calculated to prompt a desired autopilot reaction: aim.

Other tendencies are the result of conditioning...

I will ask students questions. Those wanting to answer raise their hands. I have asked them, "Why did you raise your hands? Why didn't you stand or respond by saying 'I do'?" Uniformly, they answer, "Because I have always raised my hand."

Telling men to "STAND CLOSE" won't do the trick. But men will naturally take time to aim when presented with a target.

Students are conditioned to raise their hands when answering a question.

"While the individual man is an insoluble puzzle, in the aggregate he becomes a mathematical certainty. You can, for example, never foretell what any one man will do, but you can say with precision what an average number will be up to. Individuals vary, but percentages remain constant," advises Sherlock Holmes in *The Sign of Four*.

People aren't influenced in the abstract. People don't make decisions in the abstract. There are always reasons. Sometimes logical, sometimes emotional. Sometimes the product of the highly predictable subconscious, emotion-driven tendencies of which Holmes spoke.

Tendencies are predispositions. The predictable way we go about satisfying our emotional needs. When you call on *tendency action plays* (TAPs) to trigger and stimulate the other guy's highly predictable emotional needs, you're *directing* rather than *confronting*. It's your argument's desired outcome that satisfies the needs you've triggered.

Here's how to TAP into those needs...

TAP #1: *"Fleeting opportunity" power.*

We have a need to get or see what will soon be gone.

A barrage of billboards urged me to take the family to Disneyland to catch the final season of the Main Street Electrical Parade before it "glows away." Disney took a 24-year-old attraction and created our family's sense of urgency to see it. When other theme parks were spending big-time bucks on new rides to lure summer crowds, Disneyland was packing 'em in to see its faithful workhorse plod its farewell trek down Main Street. (The Electrical Parade did "glow away," but a few seasons later it was back in Anaheim at Disney's California Adventure. So much for Disney's credibility.)

When was the last time you visited a museum? If you're like me, it was probably to catch a temporary exhibit. Traveling museum exhibits (Fabergé eggs and the jewels of the Romanovs, for example) are more profitable and more popular than permanent exhibits that often are much more impressive. Viewers who haven't visited their museum's permanent exhibitions in years rush to see touring exhibits, knowing that they'll soon be packing up and hitting the road.

Auctioneers are masters of the "glow away" tactic. Here's how a successful Los Angeles art auctioneer owned up to the secret of his success:

> Make the auction go quickly. Keep the clock ticking. Keep the environment kinetic. Don't give bidders a lot of time to think between bids. Create a "last chance" feeling that unless immediate action is taken, the item could be lost to another.

When I put on the khakis and leather laces, it's usually with a Hawaiian-style shirt. Shirts that remind me to kick back. Shirts so in-your-face colorful that I know the coat-and-tie part of my week is over.

I know my Hawaiian shirts. On Maui, every other shop sells Hawaiian shirts. The ones that don't sell them sell chocolate-covered macadamia nuts. The shirts and the nuts are my two island vices. As I was thumbing through a center-aisle shirt rack, the clerk pointed to a rack off to the side. "These patterns are flyin' out the door," he proudly declared. I knew better. Their flyin' days were over lotsa luaus ago.

It was a coat-and-tie day when I met with "Scott," a successful home builder, in his Arizona office. A plaster topographic model of Scott's latest project showed prospective buyers where streets and houses would soon be built. Scott's model was dotted with itty-bitty trees, cars, greenbelts, and "sold" flags.

"We really haven't sold this many houses," Scott confided as he pointed to the itty-bitty "sold" flags. "But they should heat things up."

"The X Factor. It's the one unpredictable element that can put the kibosh on even the most brilliant of fleeting opportunity pitches. That factor is inertia," writes *Entrepreneur*.

Inertia is the propensity people have not to take action. It's possible that the other person may find your argument convincing but not respond to your call for action for no reason other than sheer inertia. Hard to swallow, but true. Inertia is one of the most powerful phenomena in the world of influence.

The X Factor is the wall magazine publishers hit when readers don't renew their subscriptions. Not because they no longer want the magazine, but because of the X Factor. In this instance, the antidote to the X Factor is the "promptness bonus"—the gift, extra issue, or special discount you earn by ordering or renewing within a specified time period.

Don't overlook the X Factor. People by their nature are slow to change or take action. But what is rewarded gets done.

TAP

Tap into the other guy's need to take advantage of your argument's fleeting opportunities. And remember, what is rewarded gets done.

TAP #2: *Having "what's hard to come by" power.*

Members and Non-Members only.
—Sign Outside the Mandinga Disco in
Mexico's Hotel Emporio

Scarcity imparts perceived value. Dorothy's ruby slippers from *The Wizard of Oz* sold for $165,000. The bullwhip used by Harrison Ford as Indiana Jones sold for $24,300.

A stash of 600 or so cigars was found in a cellar where Irish dampness kept them well preserved and smokable since the 1860s. The owner turned down an offer to sell them for $2,000 per cigar—$22 per puff, according to those in the know.

John F. Kennedy's walnut cigar humidor sold for $574,500. The body tag from Lee Harvey Oswald's corpse sold for $6,600. The estate of Jacqueline Kennedy Onassis was auctioned by Sotheby's piece by piece. The auction fetched stratospheric prices, prompting the scene to be dubbed "Camelot craziness." Intrinsic value played a small part in the frenzy. Jackie's diamond, ruby, and emerald necklace sold for $156,000. It was resold two years later—this time without the hoopla or hype—for $74,000, a 53 percent plunge from the stratosphere.

On New York's Madison Avenue, I saw a street merchant selling watches from a case resting on a collapsible stand. Two blocks away, another watch vendor was similarly fixturized for business. Most people walked by the first vendor without missing a beat, but stopped to glance at the second vendor's wares. The difference? The first vendor's watches were jammed together sardine-style. The second vendor only had six watches on display. He had created an appearance of scarcity.

I had a few hours to kill before heading to the Las Vegas airport and home. Those few hours left me with two choices: gamble or shop. I opted for the shopping. Even pricey stores are a better bet than craps. I headed to the Ralph Lauren Polo store in Caesar's Forum Shops.

On an antique table in the middle of the store were five ties perfectly laid out side by side. They were the same except for the color of their stripes. A very different red-orange/bright-blue combination caught my eye. While standing at the cash register, I noticed the tie had a snag. "No problem," a salesperson said. "Let's go over to the tie drawer."

The open drawer revealed a chaotic jumble of about 40 striped ties. Many the same as the one I had chosen. She pulled a tie from the scramble and carefully smoothed it out. Too late. I was turned off the minute the drawer was pulled open. Before going to the tie drawer, my choice was unique, but now it was just another tie. All the smoothing out and tissue-paper wrapping in the world wasn't going to change that. How we look at everything in life—a New York street vendor's not-so-fine watches, Polo's fine ties, your argument—is a matter of presentation.

I'm not alone in how I felt. Shopping mall stores find that by displaying fewer clothes, they encourage full-price purchases. "If there's a jacket you love and you see only six on a rack, you're more likely to pay full price for it," strategizes an Ann Taylor stores executive.

And while we're on the fashion scene, remember the little green Lacoste crocodile? At one time the logo only appeared on the finest of cotton knit shirts. But then General Mills bought the Lacoste brand, and soon the croc was appearing on polyester schlock. By the mid-1980s, the logo had little cachet—the victim of overexposure on discounter's racks.

The Lacoste family came to the croc's rescue. The brand is back under their control. You may have trouble spotting the croc though. He can only be spotted in the best of stores and only on the likes of expensive knit shirts and sweaters. The Lacoste family's save-the-croc strategy: make something less accessible and it becomes more desirable.

And now for some fashion news about the teensy-weensy black bikini: Chanel, the Paris fashion house, introduced the black "eye patch" bikini, named for the approximate area of breast coverage. Only the bikini is teensy-weensy. The tab: $500. When asked about the price, a Chanel publicist explained, "It's based on the fact that you won't see every woman wearing it. It's a very special thing."

Triumph, the Japanese lingerie-maker, celebrated soccer's World Cup with 100 limited-edition bras that had soccer balls printed on the cups. The $130 bras were a sellout.

Or consider baseball cards: Hockey Hall of Famer Wayne Gretzky sold his 1909 Honus Wagner baseball card for $1,270,000 on an Internet auction. It was one of an estimated 50 that remain. Another owner stated he would be glad to rent you his Honus Wagner for $100,000 a year. "We're not talking Matisse here, but we're talking Matisse prices. The printing and paper are not worthy of the cards being catapulted to any kind of an exalted status. As collectibles for investment, baseball cards have never made sense. You buy inflated goods...then hope some other fool will come along and pay you even more," warns *Forbes*.

It's called the "Coors Effect." In the 1970s, Coors beer was only available in parts of the West. Because people want what they can't get, a cult following for the beer developed on campuses elsewhere. East Coast students were known to drive hundreds of miles to buy a case of Coors. In the 1980s, Coors became available nationwide—the Coors cult quickly evaporated as Coors became just another easily gotten brew.

Krispy Kreme suffered the Coors Effect. In late 2000, a Krispy Kreme store opened in Rochester, New York. By 5 a.m., more than 100 people were lined up in a snowstorm to be among the first to get a sugary sweet doughnut hot off the conveyor belt. By 6 a.m., 75 cars were clogging the drive-through lane. The "newsworthy" event was played out on three television stations and live radio. The excitement was real—Krispy Kreme had come to Rochester. But Krispy Kreme grew so quickly that it soon lost its cult status. Today, you can buy the doughnuts at grocery stores, where you fill your gas tank, and in self-serve display cases. "Doughnut theater," where anxious customers watch behind glass as doughnuts are cooked and then splashed with white glaze, just isn't exciting "theater" anymore.

TAP

Tap into the other person's need to have what's not easily gotten. Create an aura of scarcity. What is hard to come by has a greater value than what is easily gotten. Availability is a yardstick of quality. It's what we can't get that we want most of all.

TAP #3: *"Need to reciprocate" power.*

> ### Quick Quiz
>
> A couple you hardly know invites you to their daughter's June wedding. Your own daughter will be getting married over the Fourth of July weekend. Are you going to feel obligated to invite this couple to your daughter's wedding?

Years ago, my folks decided to sell their home and move to a condo. They interviewed salespeople from the area's two largest Realtors and were duly impressed by both. I recommended Jerry B., a young fellow who had just opened his own office. Mom and Dad liked Jerry, but they felt they would be better off with a more seasoned pro.

I was surprised to learn that Jerry bagged my folks' listing. Why did they change their minds? Jerry had a 6-foot salami delivered to them with a note that read: "No baloney, I'd really like your listing." Mom and Dad felt obligated to reciprocate by giving Jerry his chance. Jerry understood human nature and good deli. Yes, he sold the house. And yes, today he is one of the city's most successful real estate brokers.

You've heard this one before...

Knock. Knock. "I've got a free gift for you!" Whether it's a door-to-door salesperson's "free gift" or an Amway product sampler, people who receive something for nothing feel an obligation to buy. When the Disabled American Veterans seek contributions through the mail, their response rate doubles if unsolicited gummed address labels are enclosed with the solicitation. Maybe this need to reciprocate is because of what we're taught early on: only ingrates and the selfish take without giving back.

> ### TAP
>
> Tap into the other person's need to free himself from psychological debt by repaying it. Do something for the other guy because he's preprogrammed to reciprocate. He'll meet your concessions with concessions of his own. Use small favors to prompt large favors in return.

TAP #4: *"Fulfilling aspirations" power.*

Nike's "Just Do It" ad took a full page:

> All your life you are told the things you cannot do. All your
> life, they'll say you're not good enough or strong enough or
> talented enough. They'll say you're the wrong height or
> the wrong weight or the wrong type to play this or be this
> or achieve this. They will tell you no and YOU WILL TELL
> THEM YES.

Reebok didn't have a full-page ad, but managed to say it all in just eight letters: "We let UBU."

People want to make the most of who they are. Take the U.S. Army's recruiting slogan: "Be All That You Can Be." Or Timex's watch advertisement: "It Is What It Is. Are You?"

Ads for Michael Jordan Cologne feature a silhouette of Jordan's head on a stark, plain background. The only words are those written across the silhouette: "Go Inside." Words that are an invitation to look inside your own head.

Calvin Klein ran ads for its unisex ck fragrance as part of its "Just Be" campaign. One ad read: "Be a saint. Be a sinner. Just Be." Another ad read: "Be bold. Be shy. Just Be." Still another read: "Be a dreamer. Be a doer. Just Be."

For a while, Monica Lewinsky was a pitch person for the "Jenny Craig Changes Lives" ad campaign. "I think Jenny Craig is a great program for someone who not only wants to lose weight, but who's looking to change their life," informed the infamous intern.

In the United States, most women regularly shave to remove body hair. Not so in Europe, where attitudes about female hair removal vary from country to country. These attitudes are influenced by long-established cultural conditions and varying notions of beauty. So how did Gillette go about changing European women's belief that shaving is not just a man's work? Gillette's television campaign focused on vignettes of young women with "aspirational" lifestyles. One commercial had children on the beach caressing their pretty young mother's legs. By showing mothers what they *could be*, Gillette convinced them to reevaluate their deep-rooted attitudes about hair removal.

We live in a topsy-turvy world of job downsizing, making ends meet, and moral debates. We realize that our own personal aspirations and attitudes must be greater than the sum of our daily duties. More than ever, we need to be able to connect with ourselves. To overcome self-ambiguity. To better understand just who we are. Each of us struggles to make sense of our lives and deepen our understanding of its purpose. When your argument appeals to a person's dream of what he or she can become, your ideas will take on new and powerful meanings.

TAP

Tap into the other person's needs to make better sense of who she is. Empower her to be who she is and who she wants to be. Show her how your suggestions can turn her aspirations into reality.

Godiva chocolates come in a gold box and are marketed as "the perfect gift." Its core market is women over 35. To counter sluggish sales, the chocolate-maker launched an "aspirational lifestyle" campaign aimed at women between the ages of 25 and 35. Although the word *diva* in Italian means "goddess," in pop culture it's synonymous with pride and strength. Every woman aspires to be a diva. The new campaign plays off the brand name—Go*diva*. The chocolatier's advertising agency calls it the "you only live once" campaign, saying, "A diva feels that an indulgent lifestyle has been earned." The new aspirational tag line: "Inside every female is a diva."

TAP #5: *"Need to catch a wave" power.*

Natural shoe polishes. Natural soft drinks. Natural stuff to change your natural hair color or bronze your natural skin tone.

It seems everyone was squeezing onto the "natural" bandwagon, even when the fit was an awkward one. Alberto VO5 "naturals shampoo" contained sodium chloride, phosphoric acid, sodium laureth sulfate, and so on. Aveeno Moisturizing Lotion "for natural relief of dry skin" contained phenycaribol and dimethicone. Clairol's Natural Instincts conditioning colorant came with a warning—"Caution: This product must not be used for dyeing the eyelashes or eyebrows; to do so may cause blindness."

Operation Desert Storm introduced us to "smart bombs." "Smart" was suddenly the bandwagon link-up word as a blitz of "smart" businesses came into being. The "Smart Chopper" smartly diced and sliced vegetables. "Smart Cuts" was the place to go for a smart do. But there was also "Smart Systems," "Smart Choice," "Smart Creations," "Smart Start," "Smart Gym," "Smart Way," and the "Smart Yellow Pages."

And then there was the "value" bandwagon and its commonly found link-up names: "Valu-Pak," "Valu-Plus," "Valu-Rite," and "value-added software." The "value" craze got so out of hand that the CEO of Taco Bell in exasperation declared in newspaper advertisements, "Value has become a consumer expectation—'value' this, 'value' that. Blah, blah, blah."

To rescue ourselves from the sameness of our days, we're quick to pick up on what is "extreme." New York phone company ads touted "Xtreme dialing," and even included a recipe for "Extreme Lemonade" (just add pineapple juice). Snickers candy bars are "extremely nuts." Playing to the magic of threes, the Suzuki X-90 was pitched as "xceptional. xciting. xtreme." Boston Market restaurants featured "Extreme Carver" sandwiches. Izod, a clothing manufacturer, pitched "Extreme Leisure" sportswear. "Extreme Investing" was a *Fortune* cover story. Clairol pitched XtremeFX hair color to teenage boys.

Our friends, Mary and Ellen, are college-educated, middle-aged women with grown children. They are smart. They are wise. And they have a true sense of what things are worth. So why is it that when we got together with them a few years back, the conversation turned to Tabasco the bull, Kiwi the toucan, Zip the cat, Weenie the dachshund, and Bronty the dinosaur? And how Curly, Valentino, Peace, Glory, Fortune, and the other bears are the hardest Beanie Babies to come by?

When the fuzzy little critters stuffed with beans first hit the market, they retailed for $5.99. A few years later, collectors were boasting ownership of Pinchers the lobster, estimated to be worth $3,000; Brownie the bear, worth $4,500; and Peanut the elephant, worth $5,000.

People started to believe that the reported prices were the actual value. Ty Inc., had orchestrated a world-class marketing coup. Pulling different models off the market before the demand for that model was fully satisfied created a perceived collector's value. But as with all crazes, the price of Beanie Babies—including Princess, the teddy created in Princess Diana's memory—went into a free fall.

A *London Observer* article found striking similarities between Beanie Babies and the Dutch Tulip Mania...

In the 1630s, the price of tulip bulbs in Holland soared in one of the first financial manias on record. At the height of the mania, you could trade a single tulip bulb for two stacks of wheat, four stacks of rye, four oxen, eight pigs, 12 sheep, two hogsheads of wine, four barrels of beer, two barrels of butter, 1,000 pounds of cheese, a bed, a suit of clothes, and a silver drinking cup. One tulip bulb, the Semper Augustus, sold for today's equivalent of $50,000.

And before anyone ever heard of Beanie Babies...

By 1925, the automobile and airplane had put southern Florida within reach of anyone on the East Coast. Lured by the vision of a vast beachfront playground, speculators sent land prices skyrocketing. Lots in downtown Miami jumped $10,000 an hour some days. Armed with maps and deeds, real estate agents made sales while standing on street corners. It was only after visitors had gotten a taste of southern Florida summers (pre-air-conditioning) and a 1927 hurricane that left more than 400 people dead that the madness finally stopped.

A perceived wave can be as compelling as the real thing: an East Coast disco wanting a hottest-spot-in-town image pays fashionably dressed shills to stand in line outside its front door.

TAP

Tap into the other guy's preprogrammed need to lock-step with what's new and novel. Tune into fads, trends, and fashions. Link your ideas to what's hot—or perceived as hot.

TAP #6: *"Need to enhance self-image" power.*

Maybe you're a lot like me. If I'm buying a gift that is the same price at Macy's as it is at Saks Fifth Avenue, I will go out of my way to buy it at Saks. You get a nice sturdy box, not one of those fold-up jobs. Tissue paper folded just so and sealed with a gold sticker. And a pretty hand-tied ribbon instead of one of those stretchy pretend ribbons. It's worth going out of my way because I like what buying at Saks says about me.

Self-image ads pitch tooth whiteners, shampoos, and exercise equipment. But here's how Slim-Fast pulled out all the self-image stops: Slim-Fast's largest potential market in Europe is the U.K.—where 38 percent of the population is overweight, and where the idea of having a shake or bar replace a meal is a strange notion. To convince British women otherwise, Slim-Fast ads are tapping into their self-image insecurity by telling them to lose pounds or else lose face to their sexier counterparts in Sweden, Spain, and France. One ad is a photo of a French model with the caption, "I love British women. They make me look great." Another ad has a Spanish model and the text, "Face it, British women, it's not last year's bikini getting smaller."

To enhance their self-image, inner-city kids want boutique-chic fashion. Designer labels are now termed "aspirational brands." When rap star

Heavy D was onstage, he wore Fila. Q-Tip raps about Donna Karan. To get bragging rights in the 'hood,' designer Tommy Hilfiger gave a wardrobe to rap star Grand Puba.

Next time you're at the grocery store checkout line, look at a Pall Mall cigarette package. It carries the tag line, "Wherever particular people congregate."

Grey Goose vodka has become a top-seller despite its high price by portraying itself as the vodka of choice for wealthy people with impeccable taste.

We think of ourselves as being rational. In truth, we are very emotional. Happiness comes from how we see ourselves. We act in ways that make us appear to both ourselves and others as competent, discriminating...and "particular."

Premium "sticks"—handmade cigars containing only whole-leaf, "long filler" tobacco—have become a favored accessory for Demi Moore and Arnold Schwarzenegger. It was only natural that handrolleds have become a "cool tool" for the terminally hip or hip wanna-be.

Feeling a little down? The root of the problem may be on the top of your head, not in it. Frizzy, flyaway, lackluster hair results in low self-esteem, increased self-consciousness, and a loss of confidence. "It brings out social insecurities, and causes people to concentrate on the negative aspects of themselves," according to a Yale University psychology professor in her study with the stop-and-smile title, "The Psychological, Interpersonal, and Social Effects of Bad Hair."

TAP

Tap into the other person's need to act in ways that enhance how she sees herself. Of having class. Of being hip. Of being discriminating. Of avoiding embarrassment. Of possessing those qualities that magnify her sense of self-worth.

TAP #7: "Needing recognition" power.

In New York, you're nobody until a sandwich is named after you.

—The *Wall Street Journal*

It was years ago. I was one of three guests invited to speak to a business group. The other two speakers were well established and well known.

Before our presentation, there was an informal wine and cheese reception. The arriving audience converged on the two other guests, asking them to autograph their books and answer questions. Unknown and unnoticed, I felt like Dolly Parton's ankles.

I helped Tommy Lee negotiate his departure from the legendary rock band Mötley Crüe. So why did Tommy leave? When it comes right down to it, maybe being a drummer in a rock 'n' roll band isn't so great after all. Unless, of course, you don't mind being hidden at the back of a stage, banging cymbals and pounding drums, while the singers and guitarists get the glory and recognition.

Tommy has now gone public saying he "was starving for some attention." He had onstage cries for recognition: setting his drums on fire and hanging from bungee cords. He had that all-too-famous video of his honeymoon with Pam Anderson. But Tommy only got to step out front-and-center when he formed his own band. Tommy has achieved the recognition he quested for. He's now a singer/guitarist.

Other drummers seeking recognition have also abandoned their sticks and moved on to where the lights shine brightest: Phil Collins of Genesis and Steven Tyler of Aerosmith have moved to stage-front. As for Ringo Starr, the Beatles let him sing "Yellow Submarine."

"If he could have sung 'Let It Be,' then all drummers could have been respected," observed Dave Grohl, the former Nirvana drummer who is now a singer.

Tommy Lee and Andrew Carnegie on the same page! What they have in common is that the same lesson can be learned from each…

Through sheer savvy, Andrew Carnegie, a penniless immigrant, built Carnegie Steel, the core of what became U.S. Steel. In the process, he became the world's richest man. Here are a few examples of how Carnegie harnessed everybody's need for recognition and why he was "The Master Motivator."

J. Edgar Thomson was the president of the Pennsylvania Railroad. To capture the railroad's steel business, Carnegie went beyond the norm of wining and dining a potential customer. Instead, he employed a can't-fail recognition strategy: Carnegie built a giant steel mill in Pittsburgh and christened it the "J. Edgar Thomson Steel Works." From then on, the railroad's steel business was Carnegie's.

When Carnegie and George Pullman were engaged in a price war for control of the business of building train sleeper cars, Carnegie tried to convince Pullman that they should join forces. Pullman wasn't persuaded. Then Pullman asked, "What would you call the new company?"

"Why, Pullman's Palace Car Company, of course," Carnegie quickly replied.

Carnegie's recognition of the Pullman name clinched the merger.

When Royal Viking cruise ships sailed the seven seas, they were among the best of the best. As a cruise ship guest lecturer, I discovered some of Royal Viking's behind-the-scene secrets. The cruise line was famous for its onboard awards ceremonies. Elderly passengers, wearing jewels and sequins from a social swirl gone by, accepted awards simply for being on their 30th or 40th or 50th Royal Viking cruise. Why did they take so many cruises?

The ship's staff was coached to remember passenger names...to go out of their way...to listen, and then listen some more. Single men in crested blazers earned free cruises by serving as "hosts," schmoozing with passengers. Ship's officers in their 30s invited women with clouds of blue hair to dance. Social hostesses knew to admire formal jewelry and gowns. For many, Royal Viking was selling something the passengers needed more than an ocean voyage: recognition.

Carnegie and Royal Viking both understood that people are highly motivated by recognition.

TAP

Tap into people's need for recognition. People act in ways that will gain them recognition. Show the other person recognition—a pat on the back, encouragement, a special treat—and your beliefs may become his beliefs.

Now Cinch Things With a Call for Action
Because it's now time to clearly say what it is you want

The evening news supplies information, but has little impact on public opinion. It doesn't ask viewers to change what they think. Winning an argument is not merely about presenting information. It's about persuasively *leading* others to your call for action.

Fill in this blank:

At the end of my argument, the thing I want to happen is _____.

Your answer is your call for action.

BACK IN THE NEIGHBORHOOD...

Here's how you, when speaking at the "no multiplex" neighborhood meeting, could persuasively play your hand:

- Grab the audience's attention: *"We are at a crossroads, and I'm here to review some critical things I've discovered."*
- Bond with the audience: *"We all like going to movies, and we like the convenience of having theaters close by...."*
- Present your core argument: *"If a multiplex theater is built, our neighborhood will surely suffer..."* (and then present your three portable points).
- End with your call for action: *"As your friend, as a concerned mother, and as a neighbor, I urge you to call Councilwoman Smith. Write to Mayor Jones. Attend the planning and zoning commission meeting Thursday evening. Tell the commission you won't tolerate a multiplex as your new neighbor."*

Let's Rewind

The call for action is made only after the speaker's argument is presented. If she starts with her call, her logic may not be heard. When someone tells you a joke, do you sometimes listen with only half an ear? Are your thought processes busy mentally rehearsing a joke that you'll share in return? So, too, we all instinctively prepare mental counterarguments the moment we know what the other fellow is arguing for.

The speaker's call has two critical elements: a sense of immediacy and a very specific request. A general call is flabby and weak. ("If you agree with me, do something about it!") A winning call for action doesn't pussyfoot around.

Ronald Reagan was invited to speak at the Berlin Wall to help commemorate the city's 750th anniversary. He was cautioned not to make any Soviet-bashing, inflammatory statements about the Wall. Drafts of his speech were circulated to the State Department and the National Security Council for their review, and they were cautioned that any text too proactive would be an affront to Russian leader Mikhail Gorbachev. Their suggestion for Reagan to say: "One day, this ugly wall will disappear."

The president stood at the Berlin Wall on June 12, 1987, and declared to the world, "Mr. Gorbachev, tear down this wall!" There it was. No hopeful thinking. No euphemisms. A clear, unequivocal call for action.

Have you noticed that the new wave of advertising doesn't pull any punches either?

Advertisers have discreetly shielded consumers from what is really going on in the bathroom. Traditionally, they've called toilet paper "bathroom tissue," a phrase never used by anyone outside of Madison Avenue. Kleenex is now using the W-word. They advertise that their Cottonelle toilet paper "wipes" better than ordinary toilet paper

And advertisers have discreetly shied away from telling us what may be in our bottled water. O Premium Waters, a small Arizona-based bottled water company, has changed all of that. Its regional television spots show two outdoorsmen urinating in a mountain stream. O Premium Waters' warning: "Do you know what's in your bottled water? Not everything is on the label."

Don't Hang the Meat so High the Dogs Won't Jump for It

That's how a Texas judge cautions litigants about arguing for an unreasonable objective. Your call for action should give you a real shot of winning something of true benefit. Cast and limit your call to what's *realistically obtainable*.

And now for a little *nun*sense to make my point…

First Take:

NUN TO MOTHER SUPERIOR: Is it all right if I smoke while praying?

MOTHER SUPERIOR (*shocked*): Certainly not!

Second Take:

NUN TO MOTHER SUPERIOR: Is it all right if I pray while I'm smoking?

MOTHER SUPERIOR: Of course! It's always good to pray.

Let's say you want a raise. You're ready to meet with your boss and argue why you deserve more money. But wait a minute. Can you predict how your boss will probably respond? Is it likely she will respond, "I just don't have the budget to give raises this year?" If that's your prediction, what can you reasonably expect to gain by arguing for more money?

Now ask yourself what is realistically obtainable: *Do I have a chance to move into a different position within the company? Do I have a chance for more training? How about an overseas assignment?*

> ### Heads Up
>
> Your call for action has to be clear and unequivocal. Your core argument states what you're arguing for (for example, no new multiplex). Your call for action is what you want others to do (for example, vote No or write to your representatives).

My $50 Tip
Because silence is compelling

You've made your call for action. So far no response? You'll want to say something. But don't. Whether you call it strategic patience...*or* watchful waiting...*or* disciplined inaction...*or* just being cool, quietly wait for the other guy to break the silence. To respond to you.

On the first night of a Baltic Sea cruise, my wife and I were assigned to a dining table with three other couples who were strangers to us. It was a friendly group. By the time dessert arrived, we knew where everybody was from, how many kids they had, and the kind of work they did.

Hugh, a rancher from Montana, asked about my persuasion and negotiation seminars. He then said, "Tell me your very best negotiating tip."

"That would be hard to do," I responded.

"I don't have time to go to one of your seminars, but I'll give you $20 cash, right here on the spot, if you spend two minutes telling me your very best piece of advice."

I smiled at Hugh, but said nothing.

"Okay," Hugh said. "Let's make that $50."

Hugh then slid two $20s and a $10 right alongside my cup of coffee. "No matter what you charge," he said, "on a per-minute basis, this may be the best fee you'll ever get."

Hugh was right. And I picked up his cash.

"Hugh, here it is, my best piece of negotiating advice: there's magic in not opening your mouth."

"I don't understand."

"Hugh, did you notice how you raised your ante from $20 to $50 without my ever having said a single, solitary word?"

"Certainly you can embellish the advice a little if you're going to keep my $50."

"Well, in addition to not opening your mouth, you could try a quick shoulder shrug or a fast wince. Either one would throw a little *attitude* into the mix."

I now call the advice I gave Hugh "My $50 Tip."

You made your call for action. There is never a need to break the silence by answering your own questions...*or* filling a lull in a conversation...*or*, in Hugh's case, upping the ante by $30.

Return your mouth to its full upright position. Stop talking when you've made your call for action. You'll have an urge to talk—it is easier to manage sound than silence. But do not repeat yourself. Do not resell. Do not rephrase.

We mistakenly believe that the more we say, the more we influence. But probably nothing you can say will improve the silence. By anxiously sweetening your proposal before there is a response, you're only arguing against yourself.

If the response is a question, keep your answer short and to the point.

Meet Jay K.
Because he knows what I mean by "attitude"

After telling the story about Hugh to a group of MBA students, one of them asked, "What do you mean by 'attitude'?"

Fortunately, her question followed on the heels of my college fraternity reunion. At our reunion banquet dinner, Jay K. got up to make "an announcement and a first-time confession." Jay lived in Chicago, but he wanted to go to Cal Berkeley. His secret: he never applied for admission. Jay just signed up for classes, completed enrollment forms, and attended classes as if he were accepted. Jay graduated with us, his secret intact. We all asked Jay, "How did you pull it off?"

Jay shrugged his head sheepishly. "Attitude," he said.

Chapter Summary

People act and react in highly predictable ways as they quest to satisfy their subconscious and conscious emotional needs. The emotional need to take advantage of fleeting opportunity. To have what is hard to come by. To return favors with favors. To fulfill aspirations. To do what's new and happening. To satisfy self-image. To be recognized by others for who we are and what we do.

Tendency action plays (TAPs) trigger and stimulate those emotional needs. Cinch consent by directing the other person to your desired outcome as a way of his satisfying the needs you've triggered.

With linkage and logic in place, it's time to be specific about what it is you want the other person to do, think, or see. That is your argument's call for action.

10

Throw a "Hail Mary"

Because it's never over 'till it's over

> It's bound to happen. Not every argument will be guide-path smooth. There will be days filled with frustrating go-nowhere dead ends and exasperating drop-offs.
>
> In this chapter you'll discover how to artfully maneuver your way through the "mind-field."

Meet 3 Arguing Brothers

Because knowledge is important; but without creativity, knowledge has nowhere to go

A father and his three sons are traveling across a harsh Arab desert.

Knowing he is about to die, the father summons his three sons to his side. "I have but 17 camels. To my eldest son I leave one-half of my camels. To my middle son, one-third of my camels. And to my youngest, one-ninth of my camels.

For years, the sons argued bitterly among themselves because 17 could not be divided by one-half, one-third, or one-ninth. One day a wise man said, "Let me loan you a camel." With 18 camels now to be shared, the eldest son took one-half, which was nine camels. The middle son took one-third, which was six camels. The youngest took one-ninth, which was two camels. The sons had collectively taken 17 camels (9 + 6 + 2). No longer needing the 18th camel, the sons returned it to the wise man.

· · · ·

Be a wise man and think outside the envelope. Seek solutions that aren't limited by the apparent...or the assumed...or by the fact there are only 17 camels to divide. The person who strikes first is admitting that his creativity is "on empty" and that he has run out of ideas.

Finesse *Worth, Value,* and *Share* Differences
Because it's easy when you know how

Many arguments are over quantitative *worth*, *value*, or *share* differences.

A common mistake is to become overly committed to your stated call for action—your announced position. Recall in Chapter 1 the fate of the African coastal monkeys that won't let go of the peanut.

What if your call elicits a counter position? Without a still center, emotions and personalities wrongfully come into play. Defending your core argument becomes a matter of ego. Positional arguing without a strong fallback option is a risky game. A game you can sidestep by arguing for an *approach* rather than a *position*.

An approach can mean the difference between resolving a dispute and going to the mats. The following six surefire, fast-acting, deadlock-busting approaches can be used in a variety of situations and ways.

Deadlock Buster #1

I had negotiated the sale of a hilltop mansion in Beverly Hills. However, during the pendency of the sale, a $1 million price reduction was argued for because the geological integrity of part of the property was put in issue. The parties' experts disagreed as to the seriousness of the problem. One thing was certain: the seller wanted to sell, and the buyer wanted to buy. What could be done to resolve this conflict?

An argument avoiding *approach* was suggested. The two geologists would themselves choose a third geologist. The conclusion of this third geologist would be deemed controlling.

Consultants are called upon to settle executive salary disputes. Appraisers are often called on external criteria to resolve conflicts involving everything from antiques to business goodwill. Sometimes the deadlock-busting authority is a published reference. The Abos Marine Blue Book has the retail and wholesale value of boats. Kelley Blue Book has the value of cars.

Deadlock Buster #2

To decorate their Turtle Creek, Texas, mansion, clients T and R acquired four fine oil paintings of slightly varying values. Later, they decided to call it quits and were arguing. What would be the best way to divide this art, realizing that each painting has a special value beyond its extrinsic worth?

It was agreed one person would get his or her first and fourth choices; and the other, his or her second and third choices. If they couldn't agree on who gets which set of choices, a flip of the coin would decide.

Deadlock Buster #3

An actress and her production company employer were deadlocked over an appropriate salary for the fourth season of a very successful soap opera. How could this deadlock be overcome?

Both the actress and the company would write down their final position—how much they would pay or agree to accept. If the two figures were within 15 percent of each other, they would be averaged. If they were more than 15 percent apart, a neutral party would select the more realistic figure of the two submitted. (This deadlock buster is often called "Baseball.") This approach encourages both sides to be reasonable in the formulation of their final offers.

Deadlock Buster #4

As an alternative approach to the scenario in Deadlock Buster #3, the neutral party could write down what he or she believed was the fairest and most equitable salary. That figure would not be disclosed to either the actress or her production company, who would then write down their own final positions. The position closest to the neutral party's figure would be the salary for the upcoming season. (This deadlock buster is often called "Golf.")

Deadlock Buster #5

Clients L and A are in the midst of a divorce. Both worked for years building the family landscaping business. Each wants to buy the other's one-half interest in the business for as little as possible. They agree on only one thing: a stranger wouldn't pay top dollar for their business. How can they break this impasse and stop arguing?

One spouse (the "deciding spouse") would decide what would be both a fair price and fair payment terms for a one-half interest. The other spouse would then get to choose whether to be the buyer or the seller of that one-half interest, using the deciding spouse's price and terms.

The deciding spouse, not knowing whether he or she would be buyer or seller, would set parameters that would be realistic and fair to either side. If the role of the deciding spouse can't be agreed on, then the flip of a coin would be determinative.

Deadlock Buster #6

Jane owned a champion female Irish Wolfhound. Jane knew little about dog breeding, the care of a pregnant bitch, or what to do with a newborn litter. Paul, an experienced breeder and a new acquaintance, owned a champion male, the father of the litter. It was agreed that the litter would be shared equally.

The problem standing in the way of true romance was Jane's concern that Paul, with his superior expertise, would choose the best puppies for himself, leaving Jane with the less-desirable offspring. No one else in the state knew as much about Irish Wolfhounds as Paul. How could Jane avoid being at Paul's mercy?

It was decided that Paul would select two pups at a time. Jane would then select one of the two pups chosen by Paul for herself. Not knowing which pup Jane will select, Paul will pick the two pups with greatest championship potential with each draw.

Change to a More Friendly Level of Authority
Because sometimes it's the only way

Each level of authority has people who have their own needs for achievement, self-worth, and security. Each level has different individual roles to play out and different constituencies to court.

When Thomas Watson Jr. was IBM's chairman, he called a meeting of his top executives to remedy what he considered to be a pressing problem. The problem was a complaint from an employee who found just the right *level* to make his argument: the employee had written to Watson's mother.

Turning to different levels of authority—the store manager instead of the store clerk, the store owner instead of the store manager—will expose different *level interests* and different *people interests* and, therefore, different *patterns of resistance*. It is at the top where you will always find the greatest flexibility. The top has the risk-takers. The policy-makers. The people who are so secure in their positions that they understand the exceptions as well as the rules.

You're going nowhere when you argue to the *wrong people* about the *right thing...*

An evangelist returned home after a week of tent meetings. His wife greeted him by asking him how his sermons went. "Well," he replied, "all week long I was at my persuasive best. My sermon on Monday about charity was very well received, as was my sermon about salvation on Tuesday, holiness on Wednesday, and forgiveness on Thursday."

"What about Friday's sermon?" his wife asked.

"On Friday, I told how it was both a privilege and an obligation for the rich to give to the poor. My talk was passionate and enthusiastically received. But, alas, it was all for nothing."

"I don't understand, how could that be?"

"The assembly of worshipers was very poor," he explained.

Meet Giorgio
Because rejection is a reactive response

Rejection of your argument is a negative response. The good news is that, by definition, a response means the lines of communication are still open.

Rejection doesn't exist in the abstract. Rejection is reactive. Remove what's causing the other person to reject your idea, and you've eliminated the problem.

A rejected point or proposal can be presented again and again so long as it appears fresh and new. When I boil spaghetti at home, it comes out either too hard or too mushy. But a restaurateur friend of mine, Giorgio, makes perfect spaghetti. For years, Giorgio insisted that I'd never be able to make truly great spaghetti because my last name didn't end in *i* or *o*. I now know better. Giorgio's secret is to take a *spago* (single strand of spaghetti) from the boiling pot and throw it against a wall. When the spago sticks to the wall, it means your spaghetti is perfecto.

Family. Friends. Bosses. Coworkers. You want your link-up to be so comfortable and easy that you can keep throwing ideas and thoughts against the wall until something sticks. Call it the "Art of Hanging In."

Deal with rejected points one bit at a time. Break big problems into smaller problems that can be reckoned with individually. Separate monetary and nonmonetary segments, discussing nonmonetary first.

Tip

Rejection is overcome by advancing your argument with a positive attitude and a soft touch. Hang in by recasting your suggestions so they appear fresh. Remember, even creative nagging is still nagging.

You Can Run Though a Stone Wall
Because here are 5 keys to open the wall's door

When you're stonewalled, the other person is refusing to have a meaningful dialogue—the lines of communication are slammed shut. If you ask questions that begin with *can, can't, is,* or *isn't,* chances are you'll get a single-word response. Single-word answers don't supply insight into the other person's desires, perceptions, and needs. They don't tell us why he or she is resistant.

The keys to making that rock talk are *probing questions* designed to flesh out the concerns and motivator buttons of people who are otherwise unwilling to open up. Questions that can't be answered with the shake of the head or a single word such as *yes, no,* or *never.*

Heads Up

To ensure you neither prompt an argument nor appear confrontational, probing questions should be asked with a still center in a sincere, unhurried manner.

Key #1: *Questions that aren't questions.*

Partial paraphrasing "questions" are not questions at all. Through this play, information is elicited by paraphrasing the speaker. Consider the following dialogue:

PERSON A: Things are crazy down here and I won't be able to fill your order on Friday.

PERSON B: You won't be able to fill my order on Friday? (Paraphrased response.)

PERSON A: Well, we have this important job that takes priority.

PERSON B: Another job takes priority? (Paraphrased response.)

PERSON A: Your materials are in. But there is a bonus if we get this other job out early. (A previously hidden agenda is revealed.)

To find out what happened to his order, Person B (the listener) partially paraphrased what Person A (the speaker) had already said.

Key #2: *"What," not "why."*

Why elicits a general "because" response. *What* produces a more specific response that better reveals true needs and interests.

Why questions are intimidating and prompt a defensive response:

PERSON A: That is my final decision.

PERSON B: *Why?*

PERSON A: Because I said so, that's why.

By contrast, *what* questions elicit fresh information, on which new solutions may be based:

PERSON A: That is my final decision.

PERSON B: *What* are the reasons it is your final decision?

PERSON A: The reasons are...

or...

PERSON A: I'm really too jammed to start a new project now.

PERSON B: Under *what* circumstances would you be able to start a new project?

PERSON A: I can't do it now, but maybe in a few weeks?

Key #3: "What if."

What if questions pose soft-touch hypothetical possibilities. They aren't offers to be accepted or rejected, but rather questions to be answered. *What if* questions stimulate conversation while also supplying new information and insight into the other person's interests and goals. ("What if I were willing to wait until February to have you start my project?")

Key #4: *Statement questions.*

Too many probing questions can make even the friendliest dialogue sound like an inquisition. *Statement questions* are probing questions disguised as statements. With some luck, the right lighting, and a little makeup, they'll not be recognized for what they really are.

> EXAMPLE #1: I was wondering what you thought of my proposal. (QUESTION: What did you think of the proposal?)
>
> EXAMPLE #2: Although this makes a lot of sense to me, it may not seem like a good idea to you. (QUESTION: What do you think of this idea?)

Key #5: *What will it take to convince you.*

"What will it take to convince you that...now is the time to move...ours is the right company to do your job...my offer is both competitive and fair?"

Stone walls are often built because of the other person's negative expectations. Manage those expectations by telling her what she *expects*, *wants*, and *needs* to hear—and then, if possible, take action that is contrary to those expectations. *Expectation management* meant my telling a restaurant client's produce vendor what they needed to hear if they were to continue extending credit:

> I know my client has not been the most dependable or reliable of customers. However, he now has the management and capital necessary to operate efficiently and to pay your bills timely.

> ### Heads Up
>
> Pounding on a stone wall with more of what wasn't working to begin with will only provoke more resistance. Why smash down walls when you have the keys to the door?

What if your Hail Mary pass doesn't work? I learned a long time ago that you never wrestle with a pig—you get dirty and, besides, the pig likes it. There is no sense to keep arguing with someone who hasn't any sense. And you can call that game "Hard Ball." But never *slam* the door closed—you may want to try opening it again.

Chapter Summary

It's never over until it's over. When you're able to "hang in," you can explore imaginative approaches and pose surgical strike questions (see Chapter 8).

Rejection is a response to something you or someone else has said or done. Rejection is finessed by dealing with that "something." Stone walls have doors that can be unlocked when you have the five keys.

If all else fails, do what Tom Watson's employee did. Change resistance levels.

CHAPTER

11

Finesse Consent From Family and Friends

Because long-term relationships deserve special care and handling

> In this chapter you'll discover the way to win long-term results and preserve relationships that you can't turn your back on. So here it is: a self-persuasion strategy to finesse family, friends, and coworkers.

Recall meeting Sue? The daughter who argues nightly with her parents about homework? Let's continue where we left off in Chapter 6.

Your argument can threaten, bribe, plead, cajole, intimidate. Plays that won't cause Sue to change. Studying just to make Mom and Dad happy isn't change. Sue will only truly change when it's in her self-interest to change. When she *wants* to adopt a new attitude about schoolwork. When she *believes* it's important to study.

Self-persuasion takes some effort, but it is a long-lasting, relationship-enhancing strategy. Pretend that Sue is your daughter. Now, let's put a self-persuasion strategy into play.

Play #1: *With a still center, consider the relationship at stake.*

Sue is your daughter and she'll be your daughter for the long run.

Assume there's an equality in your relationship with Sue. Agreed, there's

151

a true difference in standing between a parent and a child, a boss and an employee, a teacher and a student. But a self-persuasion strategy is advanced by assuming a *fictional equality*. It's a state of equality that creates a *connectivity* that gives Sue the time and space to express her ideas and feelings. This state of fictional equality helps construct a Consent Zone where ideas can be tested and communications restored.

Use the 75/25 Partnering Secret (see page 59) and Question Sandwiches (see page 64) to ensure that Sue has the space to make herself truly heard. Having been heard, Sue will be more receptive to what you have to say.

A fictional equality means resisting your urge to be...

Diagnosing: "Sue, I know just what your problem is."

Judging: "Sue, that's the craziest (or silliest, worst, most stupid) idea I've ever heard."

Preaching: "Sue, you really should be...."

Disparaging: "Sue, you're still only a kid and you don't understand."

Minimizing: "Sue, you're trying to make a big deal out of it. Well, it's not."

It's important to the *persuasion progression* to hear Sue out. Try to understand how she feels. Show her you understand what it is she's telling you.

By identifying with Sue and her situation, she'll begin to feel that you'll try to work with her side by side rather than toe-to-toe. By *affecting* and *being affected*, you're creating an aura of *interactive power*. When Sue perceives you as sharing the homework/social-life dilemma, your suggestions will be given a "teammate's" consideration:

EXAMPLE: Your friends are very important to you. And I understand you feel like a study nerd whom life is passing by. I know you feel that your teachers really seem to be loading on the homework. They may not be aware of how many assignments each is giving you. But we need to talk about how the work will get done.

Play #2: *Use "I feel" statements to express how you feel and what you want.*

"I feel" statements are a *linking tactic* because they are not judgmental and can't be disproved.

Because you want Sue to understand your feelings and reasoning, what you don't want to say is, "You're not studying enough...."

EXAMPLE #1: I *feel* it's important that you study more because....

EXAMPLE #2: I *feel* that high school is really a small part of life. We all have to make short-term sacrifices for long-term goals.

Sue can't find fault with your feelings. If you tell Sue you *feel* happy, she can't tell you you're wrong. If you tell Sue you *feel* sad, she can't correct you. How can Sue tell you that those aren't your feelings?

Chances are pretty good that you have a shopping list of grievances unrelated to Sue's studying: her room is messy, her makeup is too heavy, and her ears have been pierced one too many times. Now isn't the time to unload old baggage.

Avoid absolutes such as *always* and *never*. They beg for rebuttal. Rarely will anyone *always* or *never* do a given thing.

Be current with your specifics. Focus on how you want things done now. Don't look back to find fault. It may make you feel good to say your piece ("Why can't you do a good job like your brother does?"), but low blows will only make things worse.

Play #3: *Tell Sue that your disagreement is with what she does, not who she is.*

Now is the time to restate your positive feelings about Sue as a person. Empower Sue by letting her know that you're willing to explore mutually acceptable alternatives.

EXAMPLE: I know that your friends are very important to you. And I think you know how strongly I feel about schoolwork.

Create hypothetical experiences. "Suppose we were" or "let's assume" hypothetical experiences cause involvement. Involvement is the persuasive forerunner to change.

Quest for points of agreement rather than an overall solution. Moving from agreement to agreement rather than conflict to agreement is an *approach pattern* that will increase rapport and lessen Sue's resistance. If you can't agree on specific major issues, seek an agreement in principle that can be a bridge to further discussion.

Play #4: *If a solution can't be reached, let Sue know that she's leaving you no choice other than to lay down study rules.*

It's rare that someone will admit that he is being unreasonable. Asking Sue, "Why can't you be reasonable?" or "What is your problem?" weakens linkage and invites further argument.

Act in a self-assured manner. Don't be defensive and don't apologize for your requests. Statements such as "I really don't like asking you to do this but…" forecast and prompt a negative response. A *still center* keeps you from projecting weakness that would encourage Sue to become more forceful and domineering.

By casting your warning as a question rather than an edict, you'll be less likely to draw a combative response:

> EXAMPLE: You think you should be able to be with your friends and do the things that are important to you. I feel that although studying requires time and effort, the long-term benefits are worth the sacrifice you need to make. If you won't study, what choice will I have other than to set rules and have penalties if they aren't followed?

Lastly...

If Sue is willing to study harder, motivate her with praise. The better Sue feels about how she's doing, the more motivated she'll be to succeed. Don't save the praise for A's. Let her know that you appreciate how hard she is trying:

> EXAMPLE #1: I really like the way you started your homework on time today without arguing.
> EXAMPLE #2: That paper you did on the Revolution was excellent.

If Sue isn't willing to study harder, firmly assert your position:

> EXAMPLE: Sue, until your grades improve, everything else will have to take a backseat to study time.

Being assertive is saying what you mean and meaning what you say. It's your clear *call for action*, and leaves no doubt where you're coming from:

EXAMPLE: In this house, homework is your first priority. There will
be no more arguments. You will do your homework and
you will do the very best job you can do.

The difference between being aggressive and being assertive is sensitivity. Being aggressive is "being impossible back." ("I'm sick of wasting my time trying to get you to do your homework. Can't you ever do anything the way you're supposed to?")

Let's play out the scenario...

MOM: It's time to do your homework.

SUE: I need to call Josh to tell him what happened to me today.
Just one more phone call...I promise.

MOM: It's always one more phone call. One more TV program.

SUE: You're not being fair! I'm losing all my friends because of
you. Why are you always on my case?

MOM: Why shouldn't I be on your case? All you ever do is talk on
the phone or watch TV. I'll be plenty fair when your grades
improve!

SUE: Why are you always picking on me? Why can't you just
leave me alone? It's not fair!

Mom, when you lost your *still center* (see Chapter 1) you got in your own way and lost control. Did you feel the focus shifting from Sue's responsibility to study to whether you're being fair? Sue has lured you into an argument. That argument isn't even about homework anymore. It's now about fairness.

To avoid an argument with Sue, repeat your expectation firmly and clearly no matter what Sue says:

MOM: I understand. But I want you to do your homework now.

SUE: I need to call Josh to tell him what happened to me today.
Just one more phone call...I promise.

MOM: I understand. But I want you to do your homework now.

SUE: You're not being fair! I'm losing all my friends because of
you. Why are you always on my case?

MOM: I understand. But I want you to do your homework now.

SUE: Why do you always pick on me? Why can't you leave me
alone? It's not fair!

MOM: I understand. But I want you to do your homework now.

You've avoided an argument by standing your ground. You were neither defensive of your position nor critical of Sue's.

If this stuck-in-a-groove play doesn't work, then it's time to back up your words by stating clearly and specifically what you mean and what will happen:

> EXAMPLE: The decision is yours. Each night until you do your home
>   work there will be no TV. No phone calls. No music.
>   It's entirely up to you.

Heads Up

Cast your threat with caution. Meaningless, vague threats are worthless. ("You'll do your homework and you'll do it right or you'll be one very sorry young lady!")

Sue may try to manipulate you through anger, tears, or pleading. Be consistent. Back down and your credibility will be lost. And as for making a last-resort threat? Follow the rules in Chapter 6 (see pages 104-105).

Chapter Summary

People who feel they're being talked into something can't be influenced. Self-persuasion plays make Sue feel you're working with her, side by side. Affecting and being affected. A self-persuasion argument produces long-term, relationship-enhancing results.

12

Win the War of Words in Writing

Because sometimes writing your argument is the only way, and sometimes it's the winning way

---

Reports. Memos. Letters. Putting your thoughts in writing enables your reader to reread, to absorb, and to understand—luxuries listeners don't have. We write hoping that we'll be read. But you never really know if you'll be read. Or if the reading will be anything more than a fleeting once-over-lightly.

In this chapter you'll discover the secrets of how to write an argument that will be read.

Meet Mrs. Townsend
Because it's time for you to be set free

Upright and proper, Anna Townsend referred to herself not as our English teacher, but as a "teacher of English." God forbid anyone would mistakenly think she was a teacher from England.

"The King's English." That's what Wilson High School's Anna Townsend called it. I called it excruciating—the tyranny of the pluperfects, those horrible predicates, the intransitives, split infinitives, gerunds, participles, and subjunctives. Be honest: Have you ever met anyone who claims grammar was his best subject? Or his favorite?

Mrs. Townsend's labyrinth of rules were the rules of formal expression. She had a say-it-my-way-or-no-way attitude about English. A lot of high school reunions later, I realize that Mrs. Townsend's rules are a framework, not a mandate.

From the time we have our first cup of coffee until we go to bed at night, we are assailed by persuasive writing of every kind and description. You write hoping you'll be read. But you never really know if you'll be read or if the reading will be anything more than a once-over-lightly. Writing that does get read has a style that pulls readers in, not shuts them out. Style that is expressive. Imaginative. Style that allows your personal touch to shine through. It's all possible because today's King's English is the English of Larry King, Don King, Stephen King, Martin Luther King, and B.B. King.

Okay, I've set you free. But come-as-you-are found freedom isn't a license to wear sweats to the wedding. The written word will always be a little more formal than the spoken. But it's not the end of the world to begin a sentence with *but* or to end a sentence with a preposition. Or to even have sentences that aren't really sentences. You know. Those things Anna Townsend called "fragments." You don't have to get all worked up about *who* versus *whom* and *like* versus *as*. You're not getting graded and you won't be sent to grammar re-education camp. And yes, there is forgiveness if you can't remember whether it's *none is* or *none are*.

Create a Hi-Touch Link-Up
Because convincing writing is convincing conversation in print

Arguments presented intellectually don't build trust. Trust is a reader's "good vibes" emotional response to how you are. Writers talk to readers. Let your ear guide your writing. Convincing writing is convincing conversation in print.

It's the "Does This Sound Like Me?" Test: Use words that real people use in real conversation. Advertisers hype their products as being robust, zesty, hearty, tangy. But has any conversation in your house ever sounded anything like this:

"Honey, what did you think of lunch?"

"The fruit drink was tangy, the salad dressing really zesty, and the stew was sure hearty, Dear."

> ## Heads Up
> We talk to each other in an active voice. When talking, you wouldn't say, "It is recommended by our councilwoman that...." You'd say, "Our councilwoman recommends...."

Before writing, take the time to think about what you'd say if you and your reader were arguing one-on-one. Now, say to yourself out loud what you would say if you were arguing face-to-face.

Quickly write down exactly what you said. You'll find yourself verbalizing emotions and thoughts that you wouldn't have otherwise put on paper. Don't correct your grammar. Don't move your words around. Just write down what you said, word for word.

It's only when you've run out of ideas that it's time to thumb through your notes. Some of the ideas that sounded good will come across as duds on paper. Toss those ideas out. Not all ideas will make your cut list.

Here's the hard part: not giving into your temptation to change vocabulary. Sure, formal words may better express your point, but they may also leave your argument sounding stuffy. Pretentious. A radio advertiser claims that they can give you the "verbal advantage" because a "powerful vocabulary gives a powerful impression." But winning arguments doesn't come from talking down to the other guy. Your goal is to win, not impress.

According to author Richard Lederer:

> Use small, old words when you can. If a long word says just what you want to say, do not fear to use it. But know that our tongue is rich in crisp, brisk, swift, short words. Make them the spine and the heart of what you speak and write.

Will short words make you sound like a 4th-grade dropout? Decide for yourself. The quoted paragraph you just read, from Lederer's book titled *The Miracle of Language,* is crafted entirely of one-syllable words! And here's a power-up plus: words with the same meaning become more powerful as the number of syllables decreases, 4-3-2-1. Which words in each of the following lines do you find most powerful?

debilitate > undermine > weaken > sap

accumulate > assemble > gather > stack

erroneous > fallacious > faulty > wrong

Power up with *fireplug words*—short, punchy, graphic, to-the-point utility words. Which of these brims with power?

TAKE 1: A bear cub knocked everything off the shelf, tore our
　　　　sleeping bags, and left the tent a mess.

TAKE 2: A bear club trashed our tent.

In Take 2, 18 words were reduced to six by using the commonly understood fireplug word *trashed*. By dropping 12 words, a soggy sentence became crisp and memorable.

Would you call the following sentence award-winning writing?

"Please read these materials so that you'll know what we plan to do at
the meeting."

This sentence is from a Ford Motor Company shareholder proxy statement. The statement's simplicity and the conversational quality of the accompanying letter from Ford's chairman won the automaker the Michigan Bar's annual Clarity Award.

Oh, if you're still worried that you'll sound like a dropout, try saying, "I'm just not the sesquipedalian I once was" (a long word meaning someone who is into long words).

How to Grab a Reader's Attention
Because you don't wet-noodle off the jump

Whether your argument is part of a report or memo, or a stand-alone letter, you want your argument to grab interest and create an undertow that will sweep the reader down the page.

"You have to hit people with a two-by-four to get their attention. Subtle just doesn't work anymore," advises the editor of the *Writing That Works* newsletter. It's true. Opening words should pop with energy.

"Does pink make you puke?" That's the leading question in an advertisement for Urban Decay, whose nail polishes are a far cry from traditional pinks and reds.

How do you convince the 79 percent of men and 42 percent of women who presently don't wash their hands properly after using the bathroom to start practicing basic hygiene? (Their mothers' nagging didn't seem to work, so that's out as an option.) You start by grabbing their attention.

In an attempt to do just that, the Allegheny County, Pennsylvania, Health Department found a way to grab people's attention and at the same time educate them to the real potential harm not washing their hands has to themselves and others. How? By tweaking the opening lines of famous literature and posting the results on public restroom stalls. Some off-the-wall samples:

> It was the best of times, it was the worst of times, it was the age of wisdom, it was the age of foolishness...it was the era of people not washing their hands after using the bathroom, it was the era of people eating with their hands and falling violently ill after transferring bacteria to each other. In short, it was not a very sanitary period.

> Scarlett O'Hara was not beautiful, but men seldom realized it when caught by her charm....Scarlett had frivolously not washed her hands after attending to her business in the ladies' parlor....Her delicate hands, being so unguarded...causing the unfortunate spread of an atrocious bacterial disease....

Would Allegheny County's hygiene argument have been as effective if it had simply posted signs saying, "Be healthy. Wash your hands"?

How to Sculpt and Shape What You've Written
Because the less you write, the more people will remember

The Ten Commandments are 173 words long. Abraham Lincoln's Gettysburg Address is 266 words long. How many words are in the argument you've written? No one needs to tell you that ours is a hurry-up, just-tell-me world. Be direct. Did you over-inform or over-educate? The more filler and fluff you eliminate, the more likely your argument will get through.

Did you write things that are interesting but not relevant? The executive director of a local charity wanting Bloomingdale's to put on a fashion show fund-raiser sent this solicitation letter to the Bloomingdale's CEO:

> Please find enclosed the materials that I promised you in my letter of last week. I apologize for the delay in getting these to you, but the office building out of which we work

experienced a small fire on Tuesday. No damage was done to our actual offices, but our computer system was adversely affected for a few days.

Do you think the CEO really cared about the fire, the amount of damage to the charity's offices, or what happened to the charity's computer system?

And did you write things that are relevant but not interesting? My wife and I will often take a guided tour on our first visit to a foreign city. It's our way of getting a quick handle on what the city is all about. It doesn't matter what country we are in, tour guides the world over launch into excruciating detail about events and people that no one on the tour really cares about. By the time the tour ends, we've forgotten most of what we heard—overdosed on detail.

I was putting the finishing touches on this chapter while vacationing "down under." A tour of the city of Christchurch included a visit to its botanical garden. Our guide's who-the-heck-cares tidbit: Enoch Barker was the first Government Gardener of New Zealand. Ho hum.

To carve his famous statue of David, it is said Michelangelo took a block of marble and chiseled away anything that didn't look like David. Here are three clutter cuts to sculpt away anything that doesn't look like it will advance your argument.

Cut #1: *What is the point of all this?*

Scrap the folklore and froufrou. While you want your personal style to shine through, remember that too much is too much.

Cut #2: *What's in it for the other guy?*

Edit out anything that goes purely to your own self-interest. Sure, you can make your appeal to a man's better nature, but he may not have one. A bulletproof argument tells the other guy the payoff in it for him.

Cut #3: *Are you telling the other person what he already knows?*

Telling a listener or a reader what is obvious is a drag. How many times a day do you suffer through this example:

> Hello, this is John Jones. I can't answer my phone right
> now because I'm either on another line or away from my

desk. Please leave your name, the date and time you called, your phone number, any message, and the best time to call you back. I'll call you back as soon as I can.

Cutting out the obvious reduces this message from 55 to 18 words:

Hello, this is John Jones. I'm not able to take your call. Please leave a message. Thank you.

Okay, every rule has its exceptions. And here are the four exceptions to the "Get on With it Already" Rule...

1. When you're cranking out an argument as part of a college term paper with a minimum page requirement.
2. When you're telling a compelling story as part of your persuasive pitch.
3. When too brief is simply too brief:

The *Eskimo Cookbook's* recipe (in its entirety) for boiled owl:
1) Take feathers off.
2) Clean owl and put in cooking pot with lots of water.
3) Add salt to taste.

4. When super "overkill" best hammers home your message:

On episodes like "Your Love Is Mine!" and "Explosive Betrayals!," *Jerry Springer Show* guests have been known to strip down to their underwear and divulge their most intimate secrets. Do you have even a smidgen of a doubt as to how columnist Mike Downey feels about the show when he argues that it is "...the most repulsive, rotten, slimy, dirty, disgusting, vile, grotesque, stinking, depraved, demented, dreadful, putrid, rancid, appalling, shameless, heartless, mindless, worthless, cruel, crude, creepy, nasty, sleazy, sickening piece of filth in the history of American television"?

How to Advance in a Linear Progression
Because winning arguments pass the "Moving Forward" Test

Each sentence and paragraph needs to say something different than the one that preceded it. When reasoning is repeated, readers become confused and lose interest.

You'll have an urge to repeat points, believing that if they're important, they're deserving of repetition. But repetition signals that there probably isn't much new up ahead. Whenever you write "in other words" or explain your explanation, you're really saying, "Sorry, but I didn't do a very good job of getting my point across the first time."

Mrs. Townsend circled go-nowhere-tangents in red, saying they were "detours." Bulletproof reasoning moves forward without deviating and digressing. Steer clear of detours by tying each sentence to a prior sentence and each paragraph to a prior paragraph. Examples of tying words include *further, besides, first, when, however, conversely, as a result, for example, even so, finally.*

Arguments that pass the Moving Forward Test present background information in a cause-and-effect or chronological order. Points in a strongest-to-weakest order. They limit each paragraph to just one idea or one point, and limit paragraphs to seven or eight lines tops. Don't be timid about using a one-sentence paragraph if it helps get your idea across.

How to Make Your Words Flow
Because you need to sweep the reader down the page

Arguments that flow make the easiest reading. Read aloud what you've written. Do the words trip easily across your tongue? When they do, you're on a winning track. Words should have a rhythm and sound good together. Breaks within a sentence should come at a natural point. When your words are read aloud, where will your reader pause for breath?

The inaugural ceremony is a defining moment in a president's career. John F. Kennedy wanted his address to be short and clear. (The final draft was 14 minutes long.) While his colleagues submitted ideas and drafts, the final product was distinctly the work of Kennedy himself. Aides recount that every sentence was worked and reworked until it was listener- and reader-friendly. The climax of his speech was its most memorable phrase: "Ask not what your country can do for you. Ask what you can do for your country." A phrase that became more compelling and less clumsy than an earlier draft that asked, "Ask not what your country is going to do for you...."

These drafts of the speech from the archives of the John Fitzgerald Kennedy Library show how he crafted his trip-easy address:

First Draft	Next-to-Last Draft	Final Draft
We celebrate today not a victory of party but the sacrament of democracy.	We celebrate today not a victory of party but a convention of freedom.	We observe today not a victory of party but a celebration of freedom.
Each of us, whether we hold office or not, shares the responsibility for guiding this most difficult of all societies along the path of self-discipline and self-government.	In your hands, my fellow citizens, more than in mine, will be determined the success or failure of our course.	In your hands, my fellow citizens, more than mine, will rest the final success or failure of our course.

From the Pros, 4 Tips for Passing the "Trip-Easy" Test

Check for words that end in *-sion, -ance, -ment, -ing, -ence,* or *-tion.* Convert those words to trip-easy verbs by dropping the suffix and tweaking the text for fit. For example, "The Company's argument is..." becomes "The Company argues that...." "The planners are in violation of..." becomes "The planners violate the...."

Check for the word *of* and replace with the trip-easy possessive form: "The decision of the council..." becomes "The council's decisions...."

Check for rambling phrases and replace them with a trip-easy word. For example, "At the time that" becomes "When." "At this time" becomes "Now." "At that time" becomes "Then." "Subsequent to" becomes "After." "Prior to" becomes "Before."

Check for word combinations that have a pleasing sound. Bloomingdale's is famous for placing customers' purchases in beige paper shopping bags on which is boldly printed the words "Brown Bag"—a much more pleasant sound than if they were labeled "Brown Sack."

How to Make Your Argument Look Like an Easy Read

Because what appears to be reader-friendly gets read

Take a breather.

Enjoy a cup of coffee.

It's only when you come back that you'll be truly ready for the "Total Look" Test's critical questions.

Look—don't read—at what you have on paper. Does your argument look like easy reading? Or something that has to be painstakingly plowed through? Brevity and simplicity (shorter sentences and paragraphs) put your argument within the reader's easy grasp.

How much of your writing is about you? There's a difference between showing what you're all about and egocentric "showboating." Chances are better than 50/50 that what you've written is too self-centric. Whatever it is you have to say about your company or yourself is a drag. Later on, you can validate who you are in ways that don't delay or obscure your argument. Check for "I" sentences that are often self-centric: "I feel that a multiplex...." "I think that a multiplex..." "I believe that a multiplex."

Are your points obvious so that you understand what they mean? Will the reader understand what they mean? Will both you and your reader have the same understanding of what they mean? Reality check: Points don't become obvious just because you say they're obvious. Truly obvious points don't need to be introduced by because-I-say-so words such as *absolutely, it appears that, clearly, definitely, in fact, needless to say, obviously, plainly.*

Now, double-check for bulletproofing...

Is there a "sounds right" core argument and three supporting points (see Chapter 5)?

Will it advance your argument to tell a story (see Chapter 4)? To use an analogy (see Chapter 7)? To home in with surgical strike questions (see Chapter 8)? Do you trigger and satisfy the reader's emotional needs (Chapter 9)?

Tips

Convincing writing is convincing conversation in print. A winning argument creates trust and throws off "feels right" vibes.

No one will read what you have to say unless you grab and keep their attention.

The three clutter cuts ensure that what you've written is interesting, relevant, and on target.

Move your argument forward in a persuasive progression. Repetition causes readers to become confused. "Detours" throw readers off track.

Trip-easy arguments flow and sweep the reader down the page.

When you're through, look at your argument to make sure it's brief, that it looks like an easy read, and that it has "sounds right" reasoning.

Now add some sizzle and seasoning...

Name Your Ideas

Because the right name is itself a powerful argument

An advertising agency renamed the *tinea pedis* malady "athlete's foot." Smart move. How likely are you to remember a name like tinea pedis? Could you possibly ever forget "athlete's foot"?

Cosmopolitan's cover could have named its featured recipe "5-minute chocolate mousse." B-O-R-I-N-G. Instead, they called it "5-minute chocolate mousse that will turn your boyfriend into your love slave."

In the early 1990s, the New Jersey Nets was a pro basketball team nobody wanted to see. The Nets lacked charisma, performed poorly, and had no superstars to attract crowds. The allegiance of local fans was across the Hudson River with the New York Knicks. Jon Spoelstra, the Nets president, had a mega marketing problem.

Spoelstra's marketing strategy was not to promote Nets games as great basketball, but as great family entertainment. To jump-start his "family entertainment" campaign, he suggested that the team adopt a name that conveys an image of family entertainment: the New Jersey Swamp Dragons. (The Nets arena is located in the New Jersey Meadowlands, a wetlands area.) The owners rejected Spoelstra's suggestion. "Too bad....Sounds like a winner," wrote one sports reporter.

Before a shot was fired in the war against Iraq, the Bush administration named the effort Operation Iraqi Freedom. A name that argued to the world that the war had a just cause: helping the Iraqi people. The 1991 Gulf War was named Operation Desert Shield. The name was a "just cause" argument that we were at war to protect the people of Saudi Arabia. Just cause imagery was reflected in the name given to the 2001–2002 war in Afghanistan, Operation Enduring Freedom, and to the 1992–1993 war in Somalia, Operation Restore Hope. The 1989–1990 war in Panama had a name that skipped the imagery and cut right to the chase: Operation Just Cause.

 BACK IN THE NEIGHBORHOOD...

In the anti-multiplex scenario, your argument becomes more forceful when given a name. Two examples: *"X-out the multipleX"* and *"Be a 'No Show.'"*

Craft Tag Lines
Because bite-size themes are power-uppers

When I say, "You deserve a break today," you think _____.
Car manufacturers know the value of a tag line:

> *Engineered like no other car in the world.*
> —Mercedes-Benz
> *The passionate pursuit of perfection.*
> —Lexus
> *The ultimate driving machine.*
> —BMW
> *Better engineered. Better made.*
> —Chrysler

And the bicycle people know the value of a tag line. Schwinn realized that it urgently needed to pop a wheelie to put fun back in the bicycle business. The un-Schwinn-like campaign tag: "Cars Suck."

There isn't a lot you can say about bottled water. Cascade Clear mountain springwater takes on its big-brand competitors with a wink and let's-not-be-so-serious tag lines such as "Water that's not watered down" and "Water just like Grandma used to make."

BACK IN THE NEIGHBORHOOD...

Tag lines are attention-grabbing, bite-size themes. In the anti-multiplex scenario, your argument becomes more potent by crafting a tag line. For example, *"Multiplex Is Another Way of Saying Multi-Problems."*

How do you know whether the tag line you are considering is a winner? It has to pass the T-Shirt Test. If it would look and sound good on a T-shirt, then you've got yourself a pretty good tag line.

Orange County, California, wanted the world to know that it was crawling into the black, having emerged from a high-profile bankruptcy. Its pros' advice: a memorable tag line to speed those efforts. After weeks of deliberations, the tag line chosen was "Orange County, The Perfect California." A bad tag line is worse than no tag line at all. Suggestions rejected by the tourism council: "Orange County: So A-Peeling" and "Orange You Glad You Came?"

I know you filled in the tag line blank on the previous page with "McDonalds." McDonald's introduced the tag line in 1971 and used it for four years. It was put back into service in 1981 and 1982. Seems like only yesterday? That's what tag lines are all about. Making points that stick.

Paint Mind Pictures
Because a mind picture is worth a thousand words

Impresarios of influence are artists who paint word pictures to ensure that their argument has clarity and interest.

From a committee chairman's written report: "The suggested proposal, although appearing to have merit, does not present the most viable course of conduct." Legendary journalist H. L. Mencken said it better by painting a word picture: "Just because a rose smells better than cabbage doesn't mean it makes better soup."

And from that same committee chairman's report: "It is important for us to ascertain our customer's true needs and interests rather than accept their remarks at face value." Songwriter Roger Miller said it better by painting this mind picture: "Some people feel the rain. Others just get wet."

BACK IN THE NEIGHBORHOOD...

In the anti-multiplex scenario, a mind picture can slam home a point: *"Just because a guy is fun doesn't mean you want him to move into your home. Multiplexes are fun, but that doesn't mean you want one to move into your neighborhood, down the street."*

Concrete words create mind pictures. Abstract words don't.

I was in the market for new corduroy pants, so I telephoned a local store and spoke to Richard, a salesman.

BOB: Do you have tan cord pants in stock?

RICHARD: Yes, we just got in a shipment.

BOB: Are they darker or lighter tan? Are they a yellowish tan? A reddish-tawny tan?

RICHARD: More of a brownish-greyish sort of tan. I hate to say this, but I'd call the color "squirrel."

Squirrel was the operative sensory word. My mind was able to picture the brownish-greyish color of our local squirrels and the tan Richard was talking about.

And in the what's-happening-out-there department: Macy's features Charter Club terry bath towels and rugs in a color you can visualize because it calls the color "reindeer."

We all remember Katharine Lee Bates's 19th-century imagery of "purple mountains majesties" and "amber waves of grain." But if you don't remember the following words from "America the Beautiful," it's because imagery to be effective must be easily understood and easily recalled by others:

> *O beautiful for patriot dream*
> *That sees beyond the years*
> *Thine alabaster cities gleam,*
> *Undimm'd by human tears!*

Do What Noah Did: Bring 'em in 2 by 2
Because more than two is too much

"The man is tall and thin." What is the immediate picture you got from this sentence? "The man is short, bald, wears glasses, and is fat." Did you also get an immediate picture from this sentence? Or did you have to stop for a moment and put the four adjectives together in their proper places?

Plop-Plop, Fizz-Fizz
Because "naturals" add pizzazz to your message

Even as we read silently, we *auralize*—we hear the sounds of words in our mind's ear. Persuasive speakers and writers add excitement by picking words with sounds that fit their message.

Some words have natural sounds: *beep, hush, splash, gobble, clang, yawn, clink, screech, guzzle, squeal.* The musical *Ragtime* advertises "cascading melodies." (Can you almost feel the flow and fall of music?) "It's been years since it was on TV, but no one who saw them will ever forget Alka-Seltzer's "plop-plop, fizz-fizz, oh what a relief it is" commercials.

TAKE #1: I heard the bell.

TAKE #2: I heard the bell clang.

Take 1 is lifeless and dull. But what's your take on Take 2?

Use Rhyming Words
Because reason with rhyme is more believable

It's old news. Advertisers use rhyme as a memory aid ("Fast Actin' Tenactin"). What's new is that studies reveal rhyme makes ordinary statements more believable. Consistently, a test group found a statement such as "Woes unite foes" more believable than the statement "Woes unite enemies."

"A profusion of confusion" is what Mr. Blackwell, the famous fashion critic, called the outfit Celine Dion wore to an Oscars ceremony. He could have called it an "abundance of confusion," but that would not have zoomed his message to readers.

"If it doesn't fit, you must acquit" was O.J. Simpson lawyer Johnnie Cochran's rhyming tag line as his soon-to-be-freed client barely squeezed into an incriminating pair of gloves. Do you recall any part of the trial as readily as Cochran's rhyming refrain?

Tip

Sizzle and seasoning make your argument more readable, memorable, and convincing.

Name your idea because the right name is itself an argument. Tag lines are bite-size themes that are your argument's linchpins.

Mind pictures create compelling clarity. Rhyme creates believability.

---

10 Mix n' Match Tricks of the Trade

Because power comes from positioning

Look at magazine and billboard advertisements and notice how marketing masters compel and convince through the placement or repetition of key words, not the repetition of points! When writing, you have the ability to move words and pieces of words around for a mix that powers up your argument with crescendos of emotion, focus, and emphasis.

Trick #1: *Repeat words at the beginning...*

This is the technique to use when the beginning words or phrases are less important than the ones that follow.

"Who was Dodi Fayed?" was the topic on the *Geraldo Rivera Show*. One of Geraldo's guests suggested that my client, Dodi, may have encouraged the attention of paparazzi on the night he and Princess Diana were killed. A professional spokesperson for the Fayed family persuasively argued otherwise by noting Dodi's very "protective" feelings towards Diana. Here's how he used this technique to power up his impromptu rebuttal: "They were dogged. They were pursued. They were harassed....He wanted to give her security. He wanted to give her peace. He wanted to give her space."

Trick #2: *At the end...*

Use this trick when you want to emphasize the repeated word or phrase.

It was the first game of an American League baseball championship series. A 12-year-old boy stuck out his glove and grabbed a ball that resulted in a game-tying home run for the Yankees. "We were robbed," declared Baltimore's mayor.

"Baseball is a game of breaks. Good calls, bad calls, in-between calls," was New York Mayor Rudolph Giuliani's responsive argument.

Trick #3: *Or in between...*

> Some who question the reason for this conference...let them listen to the voices of women in their homes, neighborhoods, and workplaces. Some who wonder whether the lives of women and girls matter...let them look at the women gathered here.
>
> —Hillary Clinton

Trick #4: *Repeat words from the end of one clause at the beginning of the next...*

> To be persuasive we must be believable; to be believable we must be credible; to be credible we must be truthful.
>
> —Edward R. Murrow

Trick #5: *Repeat prefixes of different words...*

EXAMPLE: Delegating unclear tasks to an uninspired, unqualified, unorganized committee will be the undoing of our program.

Trick #6: *Or repeat the suffix of different words...*

Example: Her idea was scrutinized, analyzed, minimalized, and
trivialized, but in the end, it alone made the most sense.

Trick #7: *Repeating sounds drive home a point...*

Lexus boasts being "passionate in the pursuit of perfection."

Trick #8: *Phrases using opposite words are memorable...*

The cost of living is going up and the chance of living is
going down.

—Flip Wilson

Trick #9: *A powerful pulsating effect is created by repeating one word over and over...*

No kites. No ball-playing. No running. No food. No bever-
ages. No this. No that.

—Sign on the New Jersey Shore

Trick #10: *Omitting conjunctions gives a staccato effect to your words...*

Look what happens when you omit the word *and*:

It was a night to remember. We talked. We danced. We
laughed. We cried.

But the repeated use of the conjunction *and* can also be effective:

It was a night to remember. We talked. And we danced.
And we laughed. And we cried.

Now...

Stop reading for a moment...

Take a few slow deep breaths...

Think back. Which of the 10 tricks do you remember best? Would you have been as readily influenced if the tools of rhyme and repetition had not been called into play?

Heads Up

A winning argument is always in the "basics"—what "feels right" and "sounds right" to the other person. The tricks you've discovered are the sizzle and the seasoning, never the steak.

You can add emotion, feeling, drama, immediacy, or urgency to your argument by tactically repeating and positioning key words and phrases. But overdoing it will be an oversell turnoff.

Don't Get Sucked Into the E-mail Trap
Because what's efficient may not be effective

Star Trek's Mr. Spock transfers information between himself and other Vulcans by touching skulls—mind-meld transfers that are direct and free of emotional content.

So, too, our own Information Age transfers are often direct and free of emotional content. As you become more technologically connected, the less connected you are as a life force—an animate being. Mailboxes made of pixels instead of aluminum. Texting symbols replacing words. Hi-tech connections lacking a hi-touch. In the process, are you abandoning the art of the one-on-one, the people skills that make your arguments compelling?

Always ask yourself, *What's my link-up priority?*

Here's how the persuasion pros see it....

> *Hi-tech* connecting is about *getting to*. About convenience. Speed. Brevity.

> *Hi-touch* connecting is about *getting through*. About movement. Change.

Hi-tech is *inanimate*. It is the cutting edge of soulless connectivity.

Hi-touch is *organic*. It's mystery. Magic. Power springing forth from who you are.

Hi-tech is about *cyber* smarts. About being efficient.

Hi-touch is about *people* smarts. About being effective.

Hi-tech best deals with "the stuff in the middle." The task-oriented. The fact-based. The when, where, and how of your day.

Hi-touch builds trust, resolves conflict, influences outcomes, and helps things go your way.

How will you deliver your message? Will you send an e-mail? Fax from an airplane? Drop a letter in the mail? Call for a meeting? Telephone one evening after the tumult of your day has passed?

Each communication medium comes with its own built-in, implicit message.

Want your proposal to deliver the implicit message, "This is it. Take it or leave it"? Then writing may best serve your purpose. Fax and e-mail traffic arrives with the implicit message that its text has special importance and immediacy. Regular "snail mail" conveys the more laid-back message, "There is no rush."

If feedback is more important than the implicit finality of writing, then an interactive medium—a meeting or a phone call—will be your choice. Initiating a live conversation conveys a let's-talk-about-it message. Investing effort in arranging and holding a meeting sends a stronger message that there is a desire to talk things out. If the other guy is skeptical or hostile, you will need a mode that will accommodate more detail and a greater depth of exploration.

According to James Fallows, a former Microsoft employee, in *Atlantic Monthly*, "Microsoft relies as heavily on face-to-face contact as any organization I've ever seen." It's easy to pretend you care. Or that you're concerned. But you can't pretend to be there. Sometimes the necessary complement to the Net is the 747.

Think about your own experiences with conflict. Maybe it was conflict with your spouse, a boss, an employee, a teacher, a student, a neighbor.

If that conflict was ever settled, it was probably because, albeit reluctantly, you met face-to-face to talk out your differences.

Heads Up

As you become more technologically connected, you become less "life force" connected. In our fast-forward world, we too quickly opt for what's convenient. Winning arguments isn't about what's convenient or efficient. It's about what's effective.

Chapter Summary

It takes time and effort to write a winning argument. But writing may be your only way. Or your best way because of geographic distance, impossible personalities, or complex issues. But with a written argument, you're never really sure you'll be read. Whether the reading will be anything more than a fast glance. Or whether you'll even be understood. A written argument doesn't provide in-person feedback. On the other hand, it gives the other guy the time and space to reread, absorb, and understand. So what should you do? For each instance, strategize your alternatives and decide which method of communication is the best.

13

Win the War of Words on the Telephone

Because it's becoming harder to travel across town

In this chapter you'll discover how to get a call through to the person you want to speak to. But you'll also discover that you may not want to make that call. And if a call is made or received, you'll discover the plays to put you at the top of your telephone game.

"I'd like to speak with Jim Smith."

"Let me see if he's here. I'll be just a minute."

(I am wondering, *How can Smith's secretary not know whether he's there, unless there's a secret passage between his office and the parking garage?*)

"I'm sorry, but Mr. Smith isn't here."

"Please have him call me when he returns."

"I would prefer you leave a voice-mail message."

Quick Quiz

Given the choice, will you opt for voice mail or opt for leaving your message with a secretary?

Dealing With Voice Mail

If you're calling someone for the first time, it may be to your advantage to state your reason for calling on voice mail rather than asking a secretary to deliver it for you. Voice mail is a chance to leave a compelling reason for being called back. What you don't want to do is blurt out your name and number and then hang up. Call it the "Deer in Headlights" Syndrome—voice-mail messages that sound as if the caller was caught totally off guard. If there's a chance you'll be leaving a recorded message, first jot down what you plan to say.

Leaving Your Message With a Live Person

What about leaving your message with a spouse, assistant, or coworker? Those folks will never convey your thoughts as well as you could in a direct dialogue with the person you called. The message-taker will attempt to relay your message logically, but the person for whom the message is intended for may not make his or her decisions based on logic.

If the message-taker conveys your thoughts after several hours or days, he or she probably won't remember everything you wanted said. On balance, a voice-mail message may be better than leaving your message with a live person. But read on...

Dealing With a Gatekeeper

"This is Mary Jones. I'm either on another call or not at my desk right now. Please leave a message and I'll call you back as soon as possible."

I punch zero and ask an operator, "Is Mary on another call or is she away from her desk?"

"She is away from her desk."

"Well, is she just down the hall (another way of saying "in the ladies' room")? Or is she out of the office?"

"I'm sorry. Company policy doesn't permit me to tell callers how far our staff members are from their desks."

Be businesslike in your dealings with gatekeepers—the people who first take your calls. Speak with confidence and authority, and they'll assume that both you and your message are important. If the gatekeeper thinks you're a jerk, that's what will be reported to the person you're trying to reach. My friend George lost the opportunity to land a big computer hardware contract because he flirted with a prospect's gatekeeper.

How to Sneak Past a Gatekeeper

No one likes being tricked into returning a call. Callers who leave only their first name or who talk to my assistant as if they were my best friend make me cast-in-stone resistant. I'd never do business with a cold-caller who tells my assistant that the reason for the call is "private" or "confidential."

To sneak past a gatekeeper, try calling after 5 p.m. Gatekeepers leave work about then and, with luck, your call will ring through to the person with whom you want to speak.

Heads Up

Before you place that telephone call, consider how you'll play the possibilities. Will you opt to hang up rather than leave a voice-mail message? Are you prepared to leave a voice-mail message that is succinct and compelling? Will you be better off leaving your message with a secretary or assistant? How will you present yourself to a gatekeeper?

---

5 Reasons You May Not Want to Make That Call
Because phoning is risky business

On balance, you may not want to make or advance your argument in a phone call. Here are five reasons why:

Reason #1: *It is easier to say No over the phone.*

The person you're calling is looking at plastic and cord instead of flesh and blood, so it's much easier to be told No telephonically than in person. Calls make it all too easy for the other person to verbally walk out of your argument. ("I was just running out the door" or "Sorry, but I can't talk right now. I am expecting a call.")

Reason #2: *It takes patience and effort to be a good telephone listener.*

Does your argument require a high degree of concentration? Is it important to explore needs and interests in a lengthy, more fluid dialogue?

Reason #3: *It's hard to manage silence over the phone.*

A few moments of silence in a meeting is a few moments of silence. A few moments of silence on the telephone is an eternity. Will you be able to resist the pressure to respond that is inherent in a telephone call? It is always easier to manage sound than it is silence.

Reason #4: *Telephone arguments are briefer and, therefore, more competitive than face-to-face arguments.*

Because meetings take time and effort to arrange, by their nature they're chattier and less structured. Will a more personalized strategy better advance your argument? Will a telephone conversation be more or less stressful? Will you be able to construct a telephonic consent zone?

Reason #5: *Your call may be an interruption.*

Will the other person be curt if your call interrupts what he or she is doing?

Heads Up

Consider whether alternatives to talking on the phone will better advance your argument.

If you decide to call and the person you want to speak with is on the phone, be sure to put on your PTV...

5 Ways to Have a Persuasive Telephone Voice (PTV)
Because you don't want the personality of a dial tone

On the phone, your voice is you. Whether it's filled with authority, boredom, anticipation, or nervousness, it's the first real clue about you. Here's what you need to know to power up your argument and be at the top of your game:

PTV #1: *Avoid a monotone voice.*

By letting your voice rise on important words and fall on the not-so-important ones, you will avoid being monotone.

PTV #2: *Vary your rhythm to emphasize key points.*

Many people believe they are varying their rhythm, when in fact they're merely raising or lowering their voice. Rhythm is a matter of pacing—speed.

PTV #3: *Visualize your listener.*

Instead of staring at the phone or doodling, visualize your listener. With that mental image, you'll project more of your personality.

PTV #4: *Enhance your voice by being in motion.*

If you talk while keeping your hands, arms, and body still, your voice will reflect the absence of motion. When you wave and point your hands as if your listener were seated across from you, you'll enhance your voice modulation, tempo, and overall drama.

PTV #5: *Know your conversation quirks.*

Although we're quick to detect conversation quirks in others, we aren't always aware of our own. Are you guilty of *uh-huhs* and other things that drive listeners nuts? Seemingly innocent expressions can irritate a listener when repeated over and over. If you record a few of your telephone conversations, you may discover irritating habits that sap your effectiveness.

11 Tips from the Best of the Best
Because they can make you a telephone pro

Tip #1: *Keep it short and simple.*

When you use complex sentences and big words, your listener will dwell on what you just said. You'll continue talking, but your listener will be a block behind and you won't have his or her full attention.

Tip #2: *Create mental pictures.*

To compensate for not having the benefit of visual aids, create mental pictures that your listener can visualize. One way is to ask, "What would happen if…?"

Tip #3: *You have the right to remain silent.*

Don't feel obliged to fill in conversation lulls. Use lulls to maintain a still center.

Tip #4: *Try "conversational harmony."*

Someone who speaks softly will feel more comfortable if you speak softly. Someone who speaks loudly will find you a kindred spirit if you match his volume. We are most comfortable with the familiar. People who sound and talk the way you do are seemingly familiar and, therefore, more likely to agree with what you have to say.

Tip #5: *Keep your tone of voice in check.*

If you sound angry, your listener will become agitated. If you sound calm, you'll exert a soothing influence. An irate person won't stay irate if you don't respond in kind—it's hard to be angry alone.

Tip #6: *Be patient.*

Repeated interruptions heighten tension. Interrupt only to confirm facts or to clarify a point you missed.

Tip #7: *Show you're listening.*

Show you are listening by periodically using comments such as "Yes," "I see," and "Go on." To encourage a speaker to keep talking and at the same time confirm you're tracking what he or she is saying, ask questions that begin with phrases such as "Do you mean to say...?" or "Are you saying that...?"

Tip #8: *Use the 1-2-3 Technique.*

It's easy to jump in too soon, cutting off a speaker with your remarks. By counting 1-2-3 in your head before responding, you leave a pocket of silence for the speaker to add something before you take your turn talking.

Tip #9: *Don't feel rushed.*

If you can't spare the time to talk, take a moment to acknowledge the call with warmth and sincerity. ("It's good to hear from you, Zack!" or

"Thanks for returning my call.") Then briefly explain why you can't talk and arrange a time to call back.

Tip #10: *Be in control.*

Sometimes calling back is better than taking an incoming call. When you place a call, control is yours for the taking. You have thought out what you'll say, anticipated questions, insulated yourself from diversions and distractions, and have all the necessary data and information in front of you so nothing is left to guesswork.

Tip #11: *Sum it all up.*

Conclude your call by reviewing the points that were agreed upon. When you follow up your conversation in writing, you reinforce concessions granted and ground gained.

4 Tests to Tell Whether You're Really Getting Through
Because to win, you have to be heard

You can't read body language through a telephone receiver, so asking questions is a way to gauge your listener's mood. After you've made four or five statements, ask a question to make sure you're being tracked. Winning arguments isn't about sounding good. Winning is about the other person tracking your ideas and understanding how those ideas fit into your total argument. Here are four tests to see if you're getting through:

Test 1: Is your listener making irrelevant comments?

Test 2: Is your listener asking unnecessary questions?

Test 3: Is your listener asking questions that you already answered?

Test 4: Is your listener saying, "I thought you said…" or "You never told me…."

If the answer to any of the above is Yes, watch out. You've just veered into an argument cul-de-sac.

Chapter Summary

Think about who will be answering your telephone call. Will it be a secretary? A recording device? Will you want to leave a message? Will you be prepared to leave a message?

There's a difference between being efficient and being effective. There are five tactical reasons why you may be better off not making your argument in a phone call.

If you opt to phone, have a PTV and argument-winning manner. The 11 tips from the best-of-the-best give you the winning edge. Use the four tests to tell if you are really getting through to ensure that the other person is listening rather than just hearing your argument.

14

Win the War of Words With an Audience

Because someday soon you'll be arguing to an audience of a few or many

---

In this chapter you'll discover the winning plays for arguing to an audience of a few or many. Plays that are different than those you'd use at less formal meetings.

The words you'll craft for a listener's ears are not the same as the words you'll craft for a reader's eyes. Readers can slow their pace to reread, to absorb, and to understand—luxuries listeners don't have.

Write out a rough draft of what you'll say. Even if your talk will be ad lib. Unprepared speakers who drift and digress blow their chances to score. Unprepared speakers suffer the Dan Quayle Syndrome: a speech with a beginning, a muddle, and an end. ("Hawaii is a unique state. It is a small state. It is a state by itself. It is different from other states. Well, all states are different, but it's got a particularly unique situation.")

Shuffle your draft's words and sentences around until a "script" emerges. Don't let it be a silent, lonely process. By talking out loud, you'll get the feel of your words and you'll actually hear how they'll sound to others. As you hear your words, you'll discover the emotional side of your argument. It's what energizes your talk. As you shape and sculpt your draft, you'll find yourself expressing ideas, feelings, and emotions that would have never bubbled up had you not talked to yourself out loud.

187

Don't be surprised if you find yourself stumbling over structured phrases. It's okay to use contractions such as "won't" or "shouldn't" because that's how you speak. Amateurs tend to prepare by writing overly formal talks. Instead of trying to be themselves, they are guided by some abstract notion of what a speaker should be. Overly formal words will only stiffen your natural speech patterns. Your argument should have the flow and feel of a conversation.

Oh – You Beautiful Word
Because most men are droners

Before I speak, I have something important to say.

—Groucho Marx

There's no such thing as a persuasive bore. A Canadian judge threw a case out of court because a witness was too boring: "Beyond doubt the dullest witness I've ever had in court...he speaks in a monotonic voice...and uses language so drab and convoluted that even the court reporter cannot stay conscious....I've had it."

Words are the skin of thoughts. They are abstractions—flat and lifeless. It's your job to bring those abstractions to life. Take the word *oh*. It's just a word. It's how you say *oh* that tells your audience what you mean:

- Pain: *Oh.* ("My stomach hurts.")
- A question: *Oh?* ("Is that right?")
- Excitement: *Oh!* ("Wow!")
- Boredom: *Oh.* ("How dull.")
- Disgust: *Oh!* ("Not snow again!")
- Disbelief: *Oh?* ("Yeah?")
- Exclamation: *Oh!* ("I forgot to turn off the stove!")
- Passion: *Oh.* ("I love him/her.")

It's hard to tune out speakers who are genuinely enthusiastic about what they are arguing for. Speakers who gesture well above the podium or move to the side of it. Speakers who use overstated gestures for larger audiences, understated gestures for smaller ones. Speakers who use a leap in pitch, an occasional exaggeration of tone, and changes of tempo and volume to build tension and surprise.

Meet Lee Iacocca
Because he talks plain and simple

Lee Iacocca saved Chrysler Corporation by winning support from Congress and the American people for the biggest corporate bailout in history. Here's how he explained his success:

> I've seen a lot of guys who are smarter than I am and a lot who know more about cars. And yet I've lost them in the smoke. Why? Because I'm tough? No....You've got to know how to talk to them, plain and simple.

The "plain and simple" talk to which he referred was using words to express, not impress. How do you know if a word is pompous? If you wouldn't use it at a cocktail party, chances are it's pompous. Using buzzwords, bytes, and bits with an audience that may not be as tech savvy as you will also keep you from breaking through.

Quick Quiz

You can't go to a ball game without singing "The Star-Spangled Banner." Without a stadium filled with fans singing with you, run through the words. Have you forgotten a few of them?

A New York radio show man-on-the-street poll revealed that not one interviewee knew the words to "The Star-Spangled Banner" beyond "twilight's last gleaming." Now let me ask you this: since second grade, you've sung our national anthem's phrase "O'er the ramparts we watched"—but what's a *rampart*?

My high school speech teacher cautioned our class that talks can be fatal if they aren't plain and simple. His proof? President William Henry Harrison stood outside in the rain for nearly two hours delivering his inaugural address. He died a month later from pneumonia.

Go Interactive
Because an involved audience is easily won over

People are more easily persuaded when they're actively involved. We quickly forget what we hear, but long remember what we've done. Depending on the size of the audience and your agenda, getting others to share their experiences, opinions, and observations is the way to win.

Interactive speakers with a high degree of eye contact are perceived as being more friendly, natural, self-confident, and sincere. Speakers who make little or no eye contact may come across as cold or evasive. Pauses become powerful when you slowly sweep your eyes across the room.

Tip

In your mind, divide the room into quadrants. When speaking, move from section to section, making eye contact with a handful of selected people in each section.

Go interactive. An audience remembers what they've *done* more than what they've *heard.*

Handout Alert
Because handouts can be fatal

When arguing to a small or medium-size audience, you can distribute handouts, although you may not want to distribute handouts until long before or long after you're done speaking. Handouts that are read while you're talking only detract from what you're saying. Ask any teacher. Chances are he or she knows the name Lee Canter. Lee is America's No. 1 educator. The fellow whose textbooks and programs teach teachers how to teach.

A good part of law is waiting. As Lee and I watched a room full of lawyers argue their cases, it happened over and over again. A lawyer would come forward and the judge would then pick up and read that lawyer's brief. As the judge read, the lawyer would verbally argue his or her position. Lee was shocked. He whispered to me:

> These lawyers don't know what every good teacher knows about getting through. You don't talk to people while they're reading. When you do, neither your written nor your spoken words will be fully absorbed nor remembered.

BACK IN THE NEIGHBORHOOD...

Hand out maps of the multiplex's anticipated traffic flow patterns in and through the neighborhood after you speak and answer questions. Make your argument more interactive.

Pros Use Props
Because complicated ideas call for simple demonstrations

Moses came down from the mountain bearing clay tablets. Would the impact have been the same if he simply announced without tablets, "Ten things were told to me by God. I'm here to tell you what they are"?

The nation was about to enter World War II. A single limp noodle on a plate was the prop General George Patton used to impress upon his junior officers what he expected of them. With his officers standing around a large table, the general tried pushing the noodle forward with his fingers. The noodle only squiggled and twisted. Patton then snatched up one end of the noodle and swept it across the plate. In no uncertain terms he made his point: "Gentlemen, you don't push...you lead!"

BACK IN THE NEIGHBORHOOD...

Use props. For example, play a videotape showing cars fighting to get into the Riverdale multiplex parking lot and the congestion caused by the moviegoers leaving.

I found a great prop in a T-shirt shop. To humorously drive home the point that sometimes we overlook the obvious, I held up a shirt that asked the burning question, "Why isn't there mouse-flavored cat food?"

4 Ways to Get Your Butterflies to Fly in Formation
Because you don't have to be a nervous wreck

Arguing to an audience isn't a life-or-death situation—although a dry throat, sweaty palms, and a pounding heart may make it feel that way. Here are four "relaxers" that are guaranteed to keep you from being a total nervous wreck...

Relaxer #1: *Pace yourself.*

When your talk is well in mind, time yourself. Then rehearse again, but this time take a third longer. A slower pace will slow your breathing and lessen your jitters.

Relaxer #2: *Visualize.*

World-class athletes know the importance of visualization when preparing for an event. Visualizing the execution of a perfect play gives them confidence. As you prepare to argue, imagine the situation down to the last detail—how you will stand, what you will say, where you will look, how the room and the audience will appear—and let yourself experience the anxiety. The fear won't disappear, but you'll become familiar with it.

Relaxer #3: *Know your audience.*

Get to know your audience. Arrive early to mingle with the folks who will be hearing you. Introduce yourself to as many new faces as possible. That way you won't be addressing a room full of strangers.

Take a tip from major league ball players who, one on one, will chat before a game about odds and ends or about themselves. Chitchat before a talk relieves tension and a nervous tummy.

Relaxer #4: *Use silence to your advantage.*

Wait to talk for five or 10 seconds after arriving at the spot where you'll be speaking. Just by being silent, you will seize control of time and space as your audience bonds together in collective anticipation of what you'll be saying.

3 Cures for the Common Speech
Because a speech and a bowl of popcorn have something in common

Popcorn without salt and butter is filling. It has nutritional value. But it's also boring and not much fun to eat. Unseasoned speeches faithfully convey information. They're boring and make for hard listening. So here's the seasoning: three cures for the common speech.

Cure #1: *Verbally highlight your main points.*

Layer your three portable points between simple, outside-the-box grabbers. Your audience will stay tuned in, and the portable points you need to get across will stand out.

Here are some fun and easy ways to step outside the box...

Songs: "We were global when global wasn't cool," declared the president of Cola-Cola. (The actual lyrics of the Barbara Mandrell classic are "I was country when country wasn't cool.")

Bits and pieces: Scan newspapers and magazines for items that can spice up your argument. When talking about where ideas come from, I like to tell how UCLA researchers, hoping to design a better football helmet, studied why woodpeckers don't get headaches—a neat "aside" from the pages of *FYI* magazine.

Movies: The current hits always have memorable lines. From years past: "Make my day." "May the force be with you." "Show me the money." "Life is like a box of chocolates."

Cure #2: *Your subject may be mundane, but you can't be.*

Senator Sam Ervin Jr. was best known for leading the investigation of the Watergate scandal. When he was 85, he wrote:

> Humor endows us with the capacity to clarify the obscure,
> to simplify the complex, to deflate the pompous, to chastise
> the arrogant, to point a moral, and to adorn a tale.

The humor that Sam Ervin was talking about was humor that percolates out of the context of your talk and includes the audience in the fun.

"A parrot, a lawyer, and a jockey walk into this bar...."

Don't open with a canned joke. Not even if it's funny. Unless you're a gifted storyteller, opening with a joke is risky business. If you don't get a laugh, you're standing there with egg on your face.

But if you feel you have to tell that opening joke...

President Jimmy Carter wasn't much good at telling funny stories. On a visit to Japan, he told a joke that had his audience laughing and clapping. Carter was so pleased with the response that he later asked his translator how he had interpreted the story for the audience. "I told them you had just told a joke, so they should laugh," the translator confessed.

If you tell a joke and it's greeted with silence, it's not only embarrassing, but you'll probably be thrown off your stride. But if you tell the audience, "I heard a funny story the other day...," your audience will know something humorous is coming up and will hopefully self-program to laugh.

Cure #3: *Use a great quote.*

Here's the reality. Not all quotes are quotable. Not all quotes are great. And using quotes outside your own area of competence may make you sound pretentious and phony.

"Rarely did Ronald Reagan permit himself to look or sound foolish, but the half-smile that played on John Paul's lips...gave the game away...," reported *Forbes* on the pope's arrival at the Miami airport. The pope and everyone seeing Reagan on the news that evening knew that the President hadn't read a word of Thomas Aquinas, whom he quoted.

Heads Up

Using any quote that is longer than 30 or so words is probably a mistake.

Keep your argument from being a snooze-fest by layering your core argument's points between grabbers. By using humor that isn't canned or contrived. Use humor that bubbles up and flows from the context of your talk. And use quotes that are brief, relevant, and entertaining.

Visual Aids are Not Always the Stuff of Winning Arguments
Because data overload is a turnoff

Visual aids can enhance the clarity and power of your argument. The more complex your argument, the more it helps to translate your points into a chart, graph, or other visual form. But boring numbers and text outlines don't become interesting just because they're projected on a screen or dolled up with computer graphics.

Heads Up

Put yourself in your audience's shoes. Most of us really don't want to read and absorb multiple concepts and long-winded factual scenarios.

Be honest. When was the last time you were wowed by anybody's graphics? Cool it on data overload. Keep visual aids to a bare-bones minimum, and don't read what's on the screen if your audience is at all literate. Instead, say something new. Here are two visual "never evers":

1. *Never ever* disconnect from your audience by talking to the words on a screen or flip chart instead of the people in front of you.

2. *Never ever* rely on visual aids to guide you through your speech. A visual aid is an aid—something to enrich or make your talk more vivid. Aids that overpower your oral presentation are counterproductive.

5 Tips to Tilt the Playing Field
Because a talk is like a love affair

Tip #1: *It's best to be the leadoff batter.*

If you aren't the only speaker, try to lead off. True, by presenting your argument first, the speakers who follow will be able to attack your argument. And yes, you'll be at a disadvantage not knowing what those later in the lineup will say. You, however, will have the first crack at winning over your audience—and that alone makes it worthwhile to lead off. If you can't go first, then position yourself to go last.

Tip #2: *Tell the person who will introduce you to just cool it.*

It's their nature. Introducers always over-embellish. The person who introduces you will tell the crowd how wonderful you are. Your ability to convince is sapped because the crowd will be thinking, *Can anybody*

really be all that good? She has a lot to prove before I'm convinced.
The surest way to prevent introducer over-hype is for you to write out what
you want the introducer to say.

If your credentials are weak, your ability to persuade will be less-
ened because of who you aren't. But if you speak without an embel-
lished introduction, and your audience likes what you have to say, finding
out later that your credentials are on the skimpy side won't have much
of a negative impact.

Tip #3: *Try not to use that old "I'm glad to be here" stuff.*

Open with a statement or question that reaches out, sets the theme of
your argument, and grabs the audience. After you deliver a captivating
introduction, you can, if you want, express your thanks.

Winston Churchill said, "I never say 'it gives me great pleasure' to
speak to any audience because there are only a few activities from which I
derive intense pleasure, and speaking is not one of them."

This was a precept Churchill only violated once. At the Other Club, an
informal group organized to discuss ideas and politics, extemporaneous talks
were a traditional rite. From a hat, a club member's name was drawn.
From another hat, a topic was drawn. The name drawn was "Churchill"
and the topic drawn was "sex." Churchill rose. Holding up the topic card,
he began, "It gives me great pleasure…." He then sat down.

Tip #4: *Remember, a talk is like a love affair.*

A friend of mine who is a persuasive speaker and a man-about-town
kinda guy insists speeches are like love affairs. They're easy to start, but
bringing them to an end requires considerable skill.

To give your argument a well-packaged feel, connect your conclusion
to your introduction. Here are two good ways you can do this and at the
same time keep your audience locked in: Start with a riddle that you answer
in your conclusion or open with a suspenseful story that you finish as part of
your closing. Power up your closing by briefly retelling your main points in a
fresh and memorable way, followed by your call for action.

Heads Up
You should be so familiar with your close that you can
close without looking away from your audience.

Tip #5: *Stay aloft when winging it.*

If you're called on to speak unexpectedly, the normal adrenaline rush response is to think about what you'll say to open. Instead, devote whatever time you have to how you are going to close. It's the finish that your audience takes home.

If you know there's a possibility you'll be asked to "say a few words," prepare some *elevator speeches* in advance. These are mini-talks keyed to your three main points. You should be able to start and finish an elevator speech in the two or so minutes it takes for an elevator ride in an average busy high-rise office building.

Heads Up

When winging it, your natural reaction will be to throw out nonstop, off-the-cuff remarks to keep from pausing. But pauses are good. They let you think about where you're going and what you want to say next.

To Memorize or Not to Memorize?
Because you have alternatives

He's the man they called "The Great Communicator." (We won't deny him this well-deserved title because of that blunder at the Miami airport.) One of Ronald Reagan's super-secrets was to memorize only the critical segments of his talk. Reagan's delivery appeared informal because the cement—what he said between his memorized segments— didn't have a committed-to-memory sound or feel.

Lindsey Graham, the Republican senator from South Carolina, spoke at Bill Clinton's impeachment proceedings. Unlike the 12 lawyers who preceded him, Graham didn't read from prepared text. He had notes, but he seldom referred to them. According to the *Los Angeles Times*:

> ...he kept his eyes on his listeners.... And for the first time in three days, all the senators seemed awake at the same time. At least they stopped scribbling and squirming and scanning their date books.... Perhaps Graham's plain-spoken style and fluency in understandable metaphors captured their attention....

If you must read, then make your words conversational. You want to be a persuasive speaker, not just a good reader. But consider this: A guaranteed-to-work alternative to reading or memorizing is to type out just the key words and phrases of your argument using a good-size font and bold letters. Have no more than a few words or phrases on any line. The written phrases or parts of phrases should be so brief that you can *scan* and *scoop them up* instantaneously. Words that connect phrases are clutter, so leave them out. Instead, type in ellipses (…) to separate phrases.

Because it's easy to lose your sense of time, most amateurs will rush through their talk. Type in slash marks (/) to remind yourself to pause. Each slash can represent about a one-second pause. You will have both long (//////////) and short(//) pauses. Put in lots of pauses. Pauses signal your audience to think about what you just said—that you've stopped talking so they can absorb.

With everything in place, you're now able to quickly look down, scoop up a word or phrase, then look at someone in the audience and speak. And then quickly look down again, scoop up another word or phrase, then look at someone else in the audience and speak.

A lecture circuit pro uses only the top half of each page so he doesn't have to look down. To avoid the flying-page syndrome, he never staples pages together. When he finishes a page, he just slides it to the side. He boldly numbers each page in the upper right-hand corner. If his pages get out of order, he is ably prepared to quickly remedy the situation.

Here's the opening of Lincoln's Gettysburg Address:

> Four score and seven years ago, our fathers brought forth
>
> on this continent, a new nation, conceived in Liberty, and
>
> dedicated to the proposition that all men are created equal.

What did Abraham Lincoln actually say when he delivered the Gettysburg Address? No one knows because nobody wrote down Lincoln's thoughts word for word. The opening lines you just read were from a version of his address jotted down later. We do know that Lincoln stood at Gettysburg holding—but not reading—his talk.

If Lincoln had notes, perhaps they would have looked like this:

> Four Score....7....//
>
> Our fathers....continent....new nation.///
>
> Conceived....Liberty//
>
> And dedicated....equal////

If you practice, the missing words will be there for you when you speak. So what if your talk isn't letter-perfect? Arguments aren't won with antiseptic readings. They are won by what is hi-touch and has a heart-driven color and feel.

A brochure for handwoven carpets boasts the carpets' imperfections in color and symmetry of design. It points out how imperfections are inherent in a product crafted entirely by hand. How imperfections are desired over "the uniformity of color, design, and dimensions" that you get with a machine-made carpet. Link up by letting your personality—imperfections and all—come through in your spoken argument.

Heads Up

Notes are a safety net—but only a net. Being a great reader doesn't win arguments. Being a conversational speaker does. Content is a totality. You're always both: your argument's message and its messenger.

Emergency Moves
Because there are 3 ways to jump-start a dead-in-the-water talk

Recall from Chapter 1 that people generally speak at a rate of about 120 words per minute (WPM). Our brains can process about 600 WPM—plenty of time left over for mental fidgeting. When a speaker is droning on, monotonic, and wordy, his or her audience will lapse into a fake listening mode rather than struggling to stay tuned.

Most speakers are so busy talking they miss the telltale signs that they're losing their audience. The following three red flag warnings signal that you're in trouble:

1. People are flipping ahead in their handouts.
2. People are looking around. (An interested audience will look directly at you unless they're busy taking notes.)
3. The buzz level rises. (As listeners become restless, they will start to whisper to those around them.)

And here's the antidote: three tricks to jump-start your talk and reenergize your audience.

Jump Start #1: *Pull something out of left field.*

A speaker referred to "an idea so big it was Jurassic." A luncheon speaker whose topic was "What to Do When the Internal Revenue Service Is in Hot Pursuit" asked his audience the heads-up-and-take-notice question, "Are you having sex with the IRS?" Prepare two or three relevant zingers ahead of time for use when needed.

Jump Start #2: *Toss in a pregnant pause before a key idea.*

With a seven- to 10-second pause, listeners will look at you because they're curious what you'll say next.

Jump Start #3: *Ask questions.*

Questions do more than liven things up. Their answers tell you how it's going and what your audience wants to learn down the road. ("What are some of the things you would like to know?" or "Where do you stand on this?")

Q&A Tips
Because there will always be questions

Taking questions and answers at the end of your talk will detract from your argument's close and call for action. Consider taking questions during your presentation or later informally. But if a Q&A session is required...

Tip #1: *Relax.*

If you know your subject matter well, you'll be able to answer most questions easily. You'll be more relaxed if you think of a question as an indication of interest rather than a challenge.

Tip #2: *Collect your thoughts.*

If a question catches you off guard, take time to collect your thoughts by repeating it. If you don't know the answer to a question, respond, "That's a terrific question! Let's throw that one open for discussion. Who wants to comment on that?"

Tip #3: *Use humor.*

Using humor to respond to a difficult question is risky. You never want to look like you're making fun of the questioner or ignoring the other person's concerns. A humorous acknowledgment should always be followed by a serious explanation.

Tip ♯4: *Don't drag on.*

Limit all of your answers to two minutes max. If a questioner wants more details, offer to meet with him or her one on one when your talk is finished.

Tip #5: *End on a high note.*

Winding up your Q&A session by calling for "one last question" can backfire if that question turns out to be dull, negative, or one you don't know how to answer. Instead, say, "We have time for just a few more questions," then end your argument on a high note—after the next good question.

Thou Shall Be Cool
Because you may encounter a heckler

Hecklers need to be heard. That need may be a more important need than extracting an answer from you.

Acknowledge your heckler's question, but keep your eyes away from him or her. When you lock eyes with a heckler, you're in danger of losing the rest of your audience. By reminding the audience of why you're there, you can portray the heckler as someone who is trying to build a barrier between you and your audience. ("I can address that issue a little later on, but for now I'm going to stick to the agenda and cover the points everyone has come to hear.")

But if you do decide to respond, wait and respond when the time is right for you.

4 Plays to Finesse Hostile Questions
Because you can't hatch chicks from fried eggs

A press conference reporter once asked Joe Lockhart, Clinton White House spokesman, if he could name one president that has told more lies than Clinton.

Lockhart's reply: "I don't think I'm going to take that question."

Recall the empowering secrets of a still center?

Defense Play #1: *Finesse loaded questions.*

Speak in a firm, calm, controlled voice. ("I'm glad you asked that question. Others who once disagreed with me expressed that very same concern" or "At one time I felt differently, just as you do now. But after having seen with my own eyes what's happening on the streets where there are multiplexes, I now look at things differently. Let me tell you why....")

It's a feel, felt, found approach. ("I understand how you feel. Many others once felt just as you do. They found, however, that....")

Finesse a loaded question by rephrasing it in neutral terms before trying to answer it:

QUESTION: Why did your company stop sponsoring college scholarships?

ANSWER: I have been asked why our company had to make such a hard choice?

Defense Play #2: *Focus on your bottom line.*

There is no rule that you have to respond to every point raised. You should, however, acknowledge what's been asked. Every time you answer a question, it's an opportunity to make a point—even though that point isn't directly related to the question. The *boomerang tactic* loops a question back to your core argument. ("I understand what you've said. The bottom line issue that must be addressed is....")

Defense Play #3: *Anticipate.*

Second-guess what will be asked by coming up with the questions you'd pose if you were on the other end of the stick. Then, come armed with an arsenal of your best bits—punchy one-liners, imaginative analogies, quick-to-grasp statistics, arm-twisting facts. You'll never be on the spot when you've anticipated the questions and have an arsenal of answers.

Defense Play #4: *Steer clear of hostility.*

It's your tone of voice that empowers you to control a hostile confrontation. Rather than meeting hostility with hostility, modulate your voice and tone so your response is slow, deliberated, and soft-spoken.

If a hostile questioner persists, don't say, "We're running out of time" or "I think this is getting too involved." Instead, have a positive comeback:

"That's an interesting point. Let's discuss it further during the break." Then quickly break eye contact and search the room for the next inquiry.

Chapter Summary

When providing your audience with a written argument, you're never sure whether you've broken through. With a talk, you'll get immediate feedback. But playing out your argument in a talk has its slippery slopes. Be prepared to do it right or don't do it at all.

15

Win the War of Words at a Meeting

Because PTAs, neighborhoods, and offices love meetings

> Arguing at a meeting requires having what the pros call a "meeting mentality."
>
> In this chapter you'll discover the tactics and strategies of a meeting mentality. Plays that are different than those you would use in a speaker/audience setting (see Chapter 14).

Pretend you are a PTA parent, one of a group of parents and teachers who will be meeting to discuss how the school's share of state lottery monies should be allocated. You know that some will argue for buying more computers. Some will be arguing to expand the sports program. Others will be arguing for expanding cultural enrichment activities such as museum field trips and new instruments for the school orchestra. You will be arguing for after-school tutoring programs for kids who would otherwise fall hopelessly behind in their studies.

How and when during the meeting should you argue?

The meeting will be held in the school library, where there is a large rectangular table. Where should you sit?

Should you argue early or later in the meeting?

What should you say if another parent asks, "Are you arguing for a tutoring program because your own child would benefit?" (That isn't why you're supporting the program, but it's true you have a child who would benefit.)

7 At-the-Meeting Tactics You Must Know
Because your argument starts before the meeting begins

Tactic #1: *The more people you know at the meeting, the more confident you will be when you make your argument.*

Arrive early and get to know the others who will be there. Now is the time to test the waters by approaching key decision-makers one on one to solicit their support.

Tactic #2: *People who talk more are perceived as leaders.*

Most people who have a point of view will either not speak up or will simply play it by ear. Your argument will be more forceful than theirs if you're prepared to support it and know how you'll tackle opposing points of view.

Tactic #3: *People who contribute early are more likely to have the most influence.*

Join the discussion early on. Keep your remarks short, simple, and direct. Use limited visual aids to illustrate main points. People remember more of what they *see* than of what they *hear*. Remember, you're less likely to be interrupted if you don't have to rummage through your notes, looking for back-up information.

Tactic #4: *Your points will be better understood if you ask questions.*

Questions cause people to think. A good rule of thumb: talk no more than a minute or so without asking a question. Questions can be ones you wait for the group to answer or ones you answer yourself.

Tactic #5: *Your argument—no matter how great it is—is bound to meet with resistance.*

Don't roll your eyes as if your opposer is the most stupid person on earth. No, not even if it's true. Make it easy for opposers to gracefully backpedal by sharing credit for ideas that stem from your discussion. Check out the Defense Plays in Chapter 14. They'll guide you through the wilderness and keep you on high ground.

Make eye contact. Looking down signals weakness. By looking the other fellow in the eye, he'll know you're listening. It's a normal urge to race to your own defense. But keep a still center and resist by pausing, gathering your thoughts and discussing them calmly. To appear less aggressive, say, "Let me play devil's advocate for a minute," then calmly state your argument.

Tactic #6: *Interrupting to correct an inaccuracy or make your argument will only make things worse.*

Interruptions breed more interruptions. Winston Churchill once admonished his opposer: "Don't interrupt while I'm interrupting!" Wait until the other person is done talking, and then put him on the defensive by asking, "What would you have done?" or "What's your positive suggestion?" Use surgical strike questions that point to solutions. Don't get bogged down with details, instead focus on the big picture. ("Let's stop a second and remember that the whole point of our meeting is to....")

Tactic #7: *Control is lost when you wait for others to take the first shot.*

Be in control of your own message. Tie anticipated negative arguments with why and how things can and will be different. This is how a CEO reported on a bad year to a meeting of shareholders:

> Clearly, we had some very fundamental problems. Our cost of goods was escalating, placing us ever closer to the bottom tier of companies in our peer group. Our return on investment was slipping. Cash flow targets weren't being met. Inventories were rising. The need to act was evident, and we did.... We are now very confident about the future.

Heads Up

Arrive early and solicit pre-meeting support. Make your argument early in the meeting. Ask questions that get others to think about what you've said. Don't interrupt others who have opposing points of view because they will only interrupt back.

---

10 Tactics When You'll Be Both Arguing at and Chairing the Meeting
Because you have the power to choreograph a win

Tactic #1: *Make sure the meeting is necessary.*

Calling an unnecessary meeting will make you look ineffective. Ask yourself, *Is a meeting really necessary? Can I avoid cutting into everybody's busy day by making a few telephone calls or sending a memo? Which alternative will best advance my argument?*

Tactic #2: *Limit the number of attendees.*

The more people in attendance, the harder it will be to get what you're arguing for. If you want fewer people in attendance, narrow the meeting's focus and keep your objectives specific.

Tactic #3: *Build a Consent Zone.*

Set the tone of the meeting by making good news announcements or sharing a personal anecdote that will tie into why you called the meeting.

If the attendees are strangers to each other, let everyone introduce themselves. Go beyond just asking each person their name and what they do by posing a question as each person is introduced. The question should be keyed to the purpose of the meeting. ("What is one thing you'd like to learn by being here?") A great way to get everyone to focus on how they can make the meeting productive is to have attendees introduce themselves not by their titles, but by explaining what they bring to the meeting's "team effort."

Tactic #4: *Remember the importance of setting.*

Setting is a critical component of the persuasion progression. If you want to be clearly in control, sit at the head of a rectangular table or stand facing the group. If you want to try to encourage attendees to interact, choose a seat at or close to the middle of the table.

You can appear democratic and still maintain your position of leadership if you take the end seat on one side of the table and seat no one at the head or the foot.

To reduce eye contact—and reduce open confrontation—seat your opponents on the same side of a rectangular table a few seats away from you. On the other hand, by arranging the seating in a circle, everyone will be able to see everyone easily and will feel more connected.

Tactic #5: *Keep it short and to the point.*

The attention span of the average person in a meeting plummets after an hour. Unless you want to establish a social (as well as a business) relationship with attendees, don't call a lunch or dinner meeting. Instead, devote all of your productive time to accomplishing your specific goals.

Your meeting will run quickly if it is scheduled for 11 a.m. or 4 p.m. These times are an hour before lunch and quitting time, and participants will be more likely to keep their input short and to the point.

Tactic #6: *Know your goals.*

The most productive meetings are the ones where you clearly set out your argument's goals and refer to them often. Distribute handouts well before the meeting begins. Meetings go faster when attendees already have background information on agenda items.

Tactic #7: *Keep on track.*

To keep the meeting moving, limit discussions to one agenda item at a time. When discussions veer off track, remind the group that "this is the issue we're discussing...."

If the meeting is in a go-nowhere mode (you'll know because everyone will be repeating themselves), restate the issue in contention and summarize any ground that has been covered. If the group still can't agree, or if it appears a decision would be adverse to you, table the issue.

Tactic #8: *State objections early on.*

Others are more likely to support an unpopular position if they have a chance to say their piece. You can force a decision, but you can't force commitment. Hostility is defused when participants sound their objections early on. ("Let's take some time to get objections out in the open.")

Divide big problems into smaller, more manageable ones. And take short breaks to sever old conversations and allow you to start new ones.

Tactic #9: *Show you're listening.*

Validate that you've heard the other guy by writing what he said on your notepad or on a flip chart or board.

Tactic #10: *Vote early and often.*

More will be accomplished if you call for votes early and often. It's a waste of time and energy to permit an in-depth analysis of every point. When it appears there is consensus on one of your points, vote on that item and move on to the next point.

Heads Up

Create a Consent Zone meeting environment. A lunch or dinner meeting may not best advance your argument. Let others say their piece. Vote early and often.

Chapter Summary

Put a winning move into play before the meeting even begins. If you're chairing the meeting, choreograph an outcome that will be to your liking.

Epilogue

Because now you're ready to win any argument!

If you haven't fought with each other, you do not know each other

—Chinese Proverb

No matter who you are, what you do, whatever the situation, there are bound to be arguments.

Arguing. There's the rough and tumble of the norm, the amateur's game. And then there's the pro's game of winning arguments by knowing how to make, manage, and move an argument. Knowing what to say, how to say it, and when to say it.

On our journey, you've discovered that self-mastery separates the amateurs from the pros. How you walk the valleys and how you maneuver the turns. Whether you're able to get out of your own way. An empowering sense of self-command and a constant state of assessment is only possible when you possess a *still center.*

You've discovered that a *Consent Zone* is a no-blows environment. An underwhelming aura that sets the tone, mood, and cadence of the argument to follow. It's a virtual place where you'll finesse rather than force. A place where others will be less resistant to you and your ideas.

You've discovered how to bring an in-your-face attack to a screeching halt and how to defuse hostility, anger, and aggression.

211

You've discovered that ideas presented intellectually won't persuade others emotionally. That it's never enough your argument *sounds right* (logical), it must also *feel right* (emotional). Feeling right is about how *you are* rather than how *things are*. The way to win is to blend approaches.

Likeability. *Hi-touch*: The approaches you need to get others to feel what you feel. Believe what you believe. See what you see.

Logical. *Analytical*: The approaches you need to get others to think what you think. Understand what you understand.

You've discovered that you can't win an argument with someone who feels they're being talked into something. *Surgical strike questions*, rather than allegations and assertions, win arguments as the other person discovers for himself or herself why it makes sense to do it your way.

You've discovered that the right words will zoom your argument from ho-hum dull to compelling. That just the right word is itself a powerful argument.

You've discovered you can prompt your desired response by tapping into, triggering, and stimulating highly predictable emotional needs that can be satisfied by your desired-for outcome. Planned action = desired reaction.

You've discovered that when your argument is in a letter or memo, the other person can reread, absorb, and understand. Luxuries a listener doesn't have. But presenting you argument in writing doesn't provide in-person feedback, so you cannot be sure whether you've broken through. In every instance, strategize your alternatives. If writing your argument is the way to go, you've learned how to make your writing convincing and compelling to the max.

You've discovered that there is a difference between what's *efficient* and what's *effective*. That an e-mail or telephone call may not be the best way to advance your argument. You now know how to be at the top of your telephone game.

You've discovered an argument-winning platform for achieving long-term results while also preserving relationships with family, friends, and coworkers that you just can't walk away from.

You've discovered that the tactics you'll use when arguing to a group are different than those you would use when it's one on one.

And a final note as our journey ends: Just as conflict is an inescapable part of the human condition, so too is deception. Our deceptions are tolerated when they aren't destructive and when they help reach a result that is not exploitive.

Each of us is a self-contained business. That is truer today than ever before. There is no such thing as a permanent job or real job security. You are what people say about you and what people think about you. That's your personal following. That's your portable goodwill.

Now go out there and win arguments!

Index

About the Author

Larry King, host of *Larry King Live*, says that "Bob Mayer is a lawyer's lawyer." Bob received both his business and law degrees from the University of California at Berkeley. A veteran been-there, done-that lawyer, Robert Mayer and his firm represent clients big (foreign governments, including Venezuela, for whom the first heavyweight prize fight ever held in South America was negotiated) and small, famous (some of America's best-known actors and athletes) and infamous, negotiating deals on everything from Amphitheater developments to the sale of Zero vintage aircraft.

In addition to being a professional mediator and practicing law full time, Mayer conducts "How to Be a Mediator" and "Negotiating Tips, Tricks, and Tactics" seminars and workshops that have been presented for M.B.A. and law students and for various private businesses, trade groups, and professional associations.

Mayer has interviewed over 200 of the world's masters—the legendary street and bazaar merchants of Bombay, Istanbul, Cairo, and Shanghai—gathering bargaining, haggling, and horse-trading tips for travelers headed for marketplaces around the world. When he can get away, he is a popular cruise ship lecturer who shares those secrets in light-hearted talks to cruise ship passengers bound for destinations where a marketplace mentality is a must to be a top-seeded shopper.

For more information, log onto Bob Mayer's Website (*www.TheWayToWin.Net*).